What Others Are Saying

Truth spoken in love sets you free to grow and mature in the fruit of the Spirit. In *Toppling the Idol of Ideal*, Melanie Boudreau has led us unabashedly over the physical hills and through the emotional valleys of raising children with hidden disabilities, and the truth she shares brings us into the broad plain of hope that we have in the future God desires for us as His children. Melanie's life lessons and research add to that hope for parents raising children with hidden disabilities by providing links, references, and resources to assist in our journey.

Even more, *Toppling the Idol of Ideal* is a clarion call to the body of Christ to rise once again to the higher standard of Christ, as seen through the parable of the Good Samaritan, in our daily interactions with those around us—especially in the places we gather for worship. That call, along with the resounding message of the author, is best summarized by the apostle Paul near the end of his first letter to the Corinthians: "Let all that you do be done in love."

Albert E. Hauck, PhD, Co-founder and President,
Friend of God Ministries
President,
Apostolic Intercessors Network

I want to read this book as fast as I can, and then I think, 'Wait, I really need to take it all in slowly and ponder it.' We parents need each other to bind up our wounds and to unbind the chains of the lies or despair the enemy of our soul puts in and on us. This book is fresh air to me. I am so encouraged!

Vanessa
Parent of a child with a hidden disability
Augusta, Georgia

I am extremely honored to have walked this journey with Melanie, sharing the experiences she and her family have encountered while raising two children with neuropsychiatric disorders. Her stories bring out the many challenges; the heartbreak of churches and communities of faith turning their backs; and the disappointments, discouragements, achievements, and accomplishments. Most of all, this book shows the joy and fulfillment of mothering children with hidden disabilities and watching them grow into healthy young adults despite the obstacles. Though I am a mental health professional, Melanie is one I would consult with any day on issues of Tourette's syndrome and other hidden disabilities. Her love for her children far surpasses any clinical or professional expertise and education. She has lived through it all.

I hope in reading this book, churches and communities of faith will glean wisdom from the information. I hope readers try to understand what many people have had to face "alone" because others have put their heads in the sand, ignoring these issues based on ignorance, lack of empathy, and compassion. This book should be in every church library, psychological office, and academic institution.

Gayle Rogers, Ph.D.
Founder and President of Forever Free
Author, *The Whole Soul: Rescripting Your Life for Personal Transformation*
Dana Point, California

If you have one or more children with hidden disabilities and behavioral issues, chances are you have been wandering in a dark, alternative world of parenting. Every day may seem like an endless battle fraught with tantrums and people judging you for your "bad" children. Melanie's book is a refreshing breeze of truth. It's well balanced and realistic, and it confronts some issues that few people will talk about. Melanie also provides hope, which you certainly need on this journey. Looking back, the days for my two boys with hidden disabilities were long but the years were short, and the love and patience were certainly not wasted.

Theresa Lynn Sidebotham
Attorney at Law
Telios Law PLLC
Colorado Springs, Colorado

Toppling the Idol of Ideal

Raising Children with Hidden Disabilities

Melanie Boudreau

ɑBM

Toppling the Idol of Ideal: Raising Children with Hidden Disabilities

Published by:
A Book's Mind
PO BOX 272847
Fort Collins CO 80527
www.abooksmind.com

Library of Congress Control Number: 2015904095
ISBN: 978-1-939828-27-9
Printed in the United States of America

Dedication

I wish to dedicate this book to my children:

To my firstborn, Kylie, for blazing the trail in becoming everything I could have ever hoped for in a child turned adult. I couldn't be more proud of you.

To my middle daughter, Carly, for your incredible bravery and strength of character. I believe in you. You have taught me more than any other child how to get my own life right. I owe you.

To my son, Collin. Your dad and I waited seven long years for you, and you were well worth the wait. You are becoming as strong internally as you are handsome, which is saying a lot.

Contents

Foreword

This book is a resource for Christian parents, family members, and caregivers who are coming to grips with the challenges children with hidden disabilities and their families face. As the parent of two such children and the husband since 1983 of the author of this book, I can tell you a lot about the topic. Even so, I am still learning each and every day, both at a "head" level as well as a "heart" level.

What Are Hidden Disabilities?

To be clear, here are helpful labels for some common ones[1]:

- Psychiatric Disabilities—examples include major depression, bipolar disorder, schizophrenia and anxiety disorders, and post-traumatic stress disorder
- Autism
- Traumatic Brain Injury
- Epilepsy
- HIV/AIDS
- Diabetes
- Cystic Fibrosis
- Attention Deficit Disorder or Attention-Deficit/Hyperactivity Disorder (ADD/ADHD)
- Learning Disabilities (LD)
- Medical conditions associated with hidden disabilities—examples include short- or long-term, stable or progressing, constant or unpredictable and fluctuating, and controlled by medication and untreatable

What Are the Challenges for Parents and Caregivers?

Speaking from personal experience and from observation, the challenges of parents and caregivers can include:

- Chronic and seemingly unsolvable parenting issues
- Lack of awareness of how to get help on how to parent effectively
- Marital strife and divorce
- Emotional pain and low self-esteem
- Burnout and being held in low esteem by others
- Small or non-existent circle of friends for support
- Expensive medical and professional care options
- Debt
- Social stigma of being a bad parent, neighbor, or guest

What Are the Challenges for Children?

A hidden disability in a child can exist undetected and be misinterpreted by parents and caregivers. For example, in our family's experience, what is actually a biochemical issue in a child can easily and improperly be attributed to purely a character issue, an unwillingness to exercise self-control or self-discipline, or a need to act out simply for attention.

Here are some challenges for children with hidden disabilities[2]:

- May not know they have disabilities or regard themselves as such
- May not have been diagnosed
- May not know what they need
- May know what they need but are unable to articulate it
- May feel misunderstood, ignored, or invalidated
- May suspect something is wrong but not know what it is or how to fix it

Speaking from personal experience and observation, I can tell you that it is not uncommon for children with hidden disabilities to experience many of the following challenges as well:

- Parents who don't understand them
- Peers who reject them or subject them to mockery
- Friendlessness
- Fear
- Isolation

- Low self-esteem
- Developmental challenges
- Desperation
- Academic challenges and learning disabilities
- Depression
- Hopelessness

What Role Can the Christian Church Play?

Since 1997 I have served as a business analyst and software architect for a globally oriented, not-for-profit, Christian ministry whose mission is to release children from poverty in the name of Jesus Christ. This ministry works at the edge of the ever-shifting expanse of global poverty that affects hundreds of millions of children worldwide.

A central strategy of the ministry is to partner with Christian churches that operate in the context of children in poverty. Both the ministry and the churches do so because they understand that the Christian church is God's "Plan A" for reaching the world, and in particular children, with the life and love of God. There is no "Plan B."

When children in poverty are engaged by these churches, their well-being is assessed by church staff members and, as appropriate, by caring professionals. They then are set on a path of development cognitively, socially, emotionally, academically, spiritually, and physically. I have seen the lives of many children who once were trapped in poverty change to lives filled with hope and direction for a bright future.

Likewise, the typical Christian churches near you and me have ministries for children, though the focus is on their spiritual training. Some have accommodations for adults and children with special needs, especially those with physical and mental disabilities. In the majority of typical Christian churches, however, the particular needs of children with hidden disabilities, as well as their families and caregivers, are not addressed adequately or at all. The reason is not for a lack of caring or neglect. Rather, it is largely due to a lack of awareness and a lack of understanding of the issues and the needs.

As the churches I work with in my business do for children in poverty, Christian churches can have a role in ministering to children with hidden disabilities and their families and caregivers. One goal of this book is to tackle the lack of awareness and lack of understanding of the majority of Christian churches about hidden disabilities so they can become effective ministers to those with hidden disabilities who struggle for help, hope, and the light of Christ.

This book offers insights and practical help for parents and caregivers. But possibly even more importantly, it brings the needed awareness and understanding of hidden disabilities to the people that comprise the Christian church. The life and love of Jesus Christ, as expressed in an informed and well-prepared church, can reach broadly overlooked and routinely misunderstood individuals—both the children who struggle with hidden disabilities and those who parent and care for them.

Stories, Facts, and Prayers to Equip, Inspire, and Give Hope

This book draws upon the experiences of our family's story as well as the stories of others. Melanie and I are living through challenges that are often indescribable and, in some cases, seemingly insurmountable. Our story is not finished yet, but Melanie does a masterful job of retelling some of the most challenging chapters in our lives thus far.

We often have the opportunity through normal social connections to encounter other parents of children with hidden disabilities. When the topic comes up conversationally, invariably there is a sense of relief from these parents that they are *finally* able to connect with other parents who "get it," who have "been there, done that," and who have insights and practical help to offer them.

Melanie has more one-on-one interactions with parents than we do as a couple. She draws upon her experiences raising our children as she shares with parents, sometimes single moms, who are often in the midst of crisis or just plain overwhelmed. She offers personal stories of hope, insight, and perseverance born of years in parenting and befriending parents in this unique context.

With this book, Melanie now provides information along with her stories and compassionate concern. To know her is to know that she is, first and foremost, a researcher. She loves to learn. She has spent countless hours researching the content of this book. Her greatest desire in writing it is to provide a concise resource, one that can begin the conversations on topics that sorely need to be addressed.

Melanie's formal education in the field of medical technology coupled with her shepherd's care for tending to the hearts of our children make her uniquely qualified to write this book. I can attest to her love and devotion to our children, who are undeniably blessed for having Melanie as their mom. Because she understands the issues so intimately, each chapter of this book concludes with a specially crafted prayer that is intended to bring life and hope into a space that is often a hard place for people to go in their prayer life.

In closing, and at the risk of understatement, I must declare here that our faith in God and the steadfast love of Jesus Christ have sustained us. The grace of God has been evident in our lives to get us to the point where a book like this is even possible.

It is my sincere hope that this book gives you some of the grace that God has afforded us. I know Melanie shares that hope as well.

Chuck Boudreau
Information Technologist
Compassion International
Colorado Springs, Colorado

"He comforts us in all our troubles so that we can comfort others. When they are troubled, we will be able to give them the same comfort God has given us" (2 Corinthians 1:4).

Preface

In 2013, one of the most important transitions in my life took place. I became a grandmother. I am now on the tail end of parenting my own children, and I can look back and evaluate the choices made throughout my child raising years as beneficial or detrimental. Parenting has been my most important spiritual as well as practical assignment, and as such, I am motivated to share what I have learned with others. My desire is for my insights to dampen the impact of the challenges you face and to infuse the same Hope that sustained me.

Who This Book Is for

This book is for parents who are just embarking on the journey of raising children with hidden disabilities and those who are well on their way and looking for camaraderie and someone who "gets it." It also offers valuable insights to those who love families impacted by hidden disabilities, including mental health challenges.

I feel strongly that chapter 12 is much needed to shift the current misconceptions about mental health and the Christian church. It provides the missing perspective that can aid churches in ministering effectively to those within their congregations with mental health issues as well as in creating a safe environment.

The Call to Write

When I discovered that both my second and third child had neuropsychiatric disorders, I hung up my lab jacket and career in medical technology permanently. Our struggles as a family, my research, and the resolution of many issues my husband and I faced parenting children with hidden disabilities gave me insights that I have had the honor of sharing with other struggling parents over many years. Experience speaking into the lives of other parents alone did not convince me to write this book. But when a total stranger, a prophetic minister, told me I would be writing a book "to help other parents cope in raising children with medical conditions like my son's," the minister's words got my attention. A series of spiritual confirmations followed, and I responded in obedience to our God, who is as passionately interested in your success as He has been in mine.

How to Use This Book

This book is both practical and spiritual. It covers topics such as laws impacting education and access to justice and seeking help from professionals when hidden disabilities are suspected. It also discusses suffering, intercession, and hope because our lives are integrated, not segregated, into the practical and the spiritual. What we deal with practically in our every day lives impacts us spiritually.

My suggestion is that you read each chapter like you would a devotional, stopping to focus on the prayer at the end of each chapter. Seek God for His confirmation and your response to what you have read to define needed shifts in thinking or action items. Journaling as you read is a good way to capture your fresh insights and ensure follow-though.

Feel free to share your constructive thoughts with me and the community of parents who follow my blog at *MelanieBoudreau.com*.

Acknowledgments

I express here my very great appreciation to Christy Ruscio for encouraging me for two years to commit my mentoring input to print. I now say, "You were right." And to the other Christie in my life, Christie Reed, your provision was a "God send." Thank you!

I am particularly grateful for the years of medical assistance given by psychiatrist Dr. Dawn Dawson, who helped my family navigate through its myriad of personal problems and on- and off-label use of medications. Thank you, most of all, for always believing me. You made me feel heard.

I acknowledge my gratitude as well to my friends Sandy Bingham, Lynn Sidebothom, Sue McMillin, and Katri Palonen, who opened their quiet homes to me for writing and editing——places where I could go to escape the screaming of the dirty dishes in the sink and the accumulating laundry. Undone chores are the most demanding voices in my home now.

No book is written without Herculean patience by an unsung editing hero behind the manuscript. Many thanks to Karen Roberts. I also extend gratitude to my reviewers as well: Dr. Gayle Rogers, Kelli Drury, Jennifer Miller, Vanessa Milligan, Kirsten Jack, Carolyn King, Lynn Sidebotham, Linda Andrews, Sue McMillin, Pam Decker, and Jo Ann Zepp. Dr. Gayle, your incredulous question, "Why haven't you written a book yet?" was the key admonition that unlocked the next year of writing. Further counsel and encouragement propelled me through to completion. Thank you! Thank you also to the publisher, A Book's Mind, for the vote of confidence that gave me the courage to write this book.

My extended family has always provided for me unending compassion and support, with no distinction between my own blood relatives and those I was gifted through marriage. I can't thank you enough for your love.

Last and most important, I offer my deepest gratitude to my husband, Chuck, who in his own right could write a book instructing other men on how to support their wives with excellence, even in the midst of raising children with hidden disabilities. I am your biggest fan. Your grace-filled love for me leaves me utterly undone.

Chapter One

The Unexpected

I set out to explore on foot. It was a beautiful summer day, and I had some time to kill. The auto mechanics were readying my abused Honda Odyssey to brave the wilds of Colorado once again, the van I imagined to be a Jeep Wrangler equipped with a three-inch lift kit for clearing large stones on dirt roads.

I had no intention of waiting several hours at the garage, especially since the garage was located next to undeveloped land that I had not explored by hiking. I had avoided that particular wilderness area for the past fifteen years. I'd held it in poor esteem ever since a fence post at the bottom of a spectacular sledding hill claimed my left collarbone one painful winter afternoon.

But this day was different. I was bored and had little else to do with my wait time. So I stepped out into the wilderness.

To my surprise and delight, the wildflower-strewn field with undulating hills and the occasional low-to-the-ground scrub oak held a secret just over the first easy ridge I climbed. Exposed before me lay a canyon, hewn by raging flash flood waters that had taken full advantage of the low-lying creek bed's terrain. Somehow, I told myself, I was going to get to the bottom of that 25-foot deep gorge and enjoy a pleasant walk along the creek. I imagined getting down safely would be my challenge. I was wrong.

As I followed the water's edge, isolated now from civilization, I discovered another secret of the chasm. The fertile soil that lined the steep slopes barricading the stream below was devoid of anchoring plant life. It crumbled under my feet as I tried to ascend to escape the hike I had envisioned along the creek. Forward progression was daunted by the overgrowth of Cottonwood tree volunteers that obstructed the path at the narrow base, so I sought another route. This hike was not turning out as I had expected. Ahead lay quicksand-like mud beneath an impenetrable wall of saplings; and behind was the way I had come, without enough time to retrace my steps. Not particularly physically fit, I was tired and felt trapped.

Picking my way along the creek, I was careful to avoid the areas of mud that consumed my feet like there was nothing solid beneath. I dodged the brambles that tore at my clothes and scratched my skin. Up was my only real option, but the crumbling walls on either side opposed me.

It was then that I discovered the thistle, the unpleasant, prickly plant I'd had no use for previously. It grew in occasional clumps along the steep walls where nothing else could gain a hold in land ravaged every so often by raging waters. Steadied by grasping a branch and using its clumps of green thistles as toeholds, I climbed slowly, precariously, to safety. It was exhilarating!

Life with Hidden Disabilities

As I climbed out of the canyon, the Lord gave me this picture. The parenting hike of raising children with hidden disabilities is meant to be an adventurous, beautiful challenge, full of the unexpected. But ascending requires I cling to the Branch and recognize that God offers me suffering as a positive provision to give me a leg up. When viewed and used properly, the thistles that grow along the banks of my life, suffering I have no use for, give me a toehold for the ascent out of the depth of a canyon that feels at the time much deeper than the mini gorge in the wilderness adjacent to the repair garage. In the ascent, I become a woman who is more mature and complete than I might have been otherwise.

I now see a picture of you as well in the story of my unexpected hiking adventure with nowhere to go but up. I see you passionate about exploring life, loving, and serving. Like me, you struggle gallantly in the quagmire at the base of the canyon that threatens to suck you in deeper, pull you down further. Like me, you search for the toeholds.

In the Old Testament, Jesus, the one who is coming to rescue His people, is referred to as a "righteous Branch" (Jeremiah 23:5 NIV) of a tree. That Branch is there for you as it has been for me. It can be clung to while climbing treacherous walls that would crumble under our weight.

The devastation of discovering a child has hidden disabilities, when it comes, may hit like an unexpected crumbling of a canyon wall into raging waters of a fast-moving river below. But this devastation is less understood by observers be-cause it seems to creep up slowly, with little or no warning, as unsuspecting parents and caregivers gaze out on what they envision as a flower-strewn path toward a seemingly clear horizon. How to deal with the devastation, how to navigate the challenges ahead, is what this book is about.

You may be strong, and you may be strong in the Lord, but you still need encouragement because the struggle to climb is daunting. In spite of the challenges, I have found the value of prickly toeholds and grabbed on to the Branch that enables me to scale the crumbling walls and come out of the canyon that once left me feeling hemmed in and overwhelmed. Allow me now to encourage you in our common climb, contending for the destiny of our children. Let's share the exhilaration of adventure, challenge, and success!

Some of you reading may be spectators along the banks, not the parents raising children with hidden disabilities but caring observers. You want to understand the challenges faced by parents. You care enough to exert the effort to learn, to avoid the mistakes made by so many other observers. You desire to gain insights on the struggle so that you are empowered with wisdom as to how to offer your help. This book is intended to encourage you as well.

> You may be strong, and you may be strong in the Lord, but you still need encouragement because the struggle to climb is daunting.

In the Beginning

Most of us start the parenthood journey on equal footing—unprepared, overwhelmed, and desperate for something that floats as we thrash around in what feels like water way over our heads. If we are honest, all of our parenting years may feel that way at times.

Baby making does not require parenting skill, happiness, peace with our own childhoods, anchored spirituality, maturity, or even a well-paying job. None of those things matter, at least at first. What matters is the child, the wonderful complexity of issues who is "our baby."

All three of my children came into this world with five fingers on each hand and five toes on each foot. They were smothered with kisses. But my second child was characteristically different. She was different in wonderful ways, with brilliance beyond our wildest dreams, doing division in her head before most babies knew their colors. But I would soon discover she was different in ways that were sometimes hard to see as wonderful.

On the bright side of things, she instinctively knew what was funny. She made puns before the age of three, laughing uproariously and bringing delight to all. She was also violently volatile, shifting from joy to rage in a split second. By age five, she held the entire family hostage to her mood swings.

Initially, encouragement was absent from my family's circle of friends and small groups at church. The Bible admonishes older women to teach what is good, to encourage young women to love their children (Titus 2:3–4). But when I needed them the most, in the beginning, mentors who understood my family dynamics were nowhere to be found.

My husband and I have learned a lot since those early days of discovery, disappointment, elation, and understanding. Our faith has come far. My desire now is to use our experiences to be that voice of encouragement for other parents like us and to help by providing the tools to contribute toward what is lacking.

What Is Needed

We may not need to be told to love our children, but sometimes we need input to understand them better and love them well. In addition, we may also need reminders to love ourselves in the midst of our failures and the sometimes unfathomable suffering. Perhaps most importantly, we may need reminders to continue to love God.

> We may not need to be told to love our children, but sometimes we need input to understand them better and love them well.

Resources are more available now than they were when my children came into this world twenty some years ago. When my husband and I first started the adventure of special needs, even finding camaraderie through the library or through the Internet was still problematic. We grasped for the few books that offered both insight and hope.

I, for example, cried as I read Susan Hughes' heart-rending book, *What Makes Ryan Tick: A Family's Triumph over Tourette Syndrome and Attention Deficiency Hyperactivity Disorder*[3], struggling to find hope as I previewed a future I felt unprepared to face. I felt angry about what might be ahead for me when I read Ross Greene's excellent book, *The Explosive Child: A New Approach for Understanding and Parenting Easily Frustrated, Chronically Inflexible Children*[4]. I was not yet willing to concede my idyllic standards for what I wanted accountability to look like in my emerging family.

It's easy even for me, the author, to convince myself a book like the one you are holding in your hands isn't needed today. After all, parents are now blogging and offering their wisdom, insights, failures, and triumphs. Medical professionals and schools are becoming more and more attuned to the needs and the needed interventions. But I'm still meeting parents who are fighting the battles real time, grasping for hope, and wrestling with their faith in the ravine while facing wild beasts named Overwhelm, Discouragement, and Despair.

This book is for all of us on the journey of raising children with hidden disabilities.

Reflective Prayer

Heavenly Father,

Sometimes I forget about the beauty You intended in this adventure of parenting. And also the value You ascribe to suffering.

But it's not just me that suffers. My child is suffering, aware all too often that he/she doesn't measure up to the expectations of others, and if I'm honest, even to my own expectations. Yet no matter how unprepared I feel raising this child, the love You have for me and for my child can lead us gently to refreshing waters, hope, and an upward ascent.

As You have said in the Bible, "What is the price of two sparrows—one copper coin? But not a single sparrow can fall to the ground" without You knowing it (Matthew 10:29). So I declare Your faithful love never ends! Your mercies never cease! Great is Your faithfulness; Your "mercies begin afresh each morning" (Lamentations 3:22-23).

"LORD, be gracious to us" as a family; "we long for you." "Be our strength"; be my strength especially every morning. Be "our salvation in time of distress" (Isaiah 33:2 NIV). In Jesus' name I pray these words. Amen.

Chapter Two

Maintaining Hope

"I hate your God. I HATE your God!" screams my daughter through clenched teeth as we drive home from voice lessons. She is at a devastating low, too depressed to enjoy even her most favorite activities: writing, drawing, and singing. Since she is twenty-two years old, my husband and I had thought by now things would be better, much better. But we are still battling.

She tells me she feels like a dead, curled up wood louse, a furled pill bug waiting to disintegrate into a thousand pieces with one touch. "I can see myself doing so many things, but I collapse just coming out of my room!" she sobs. It's not only voice lessons that don't go well today. Life is not going well.

I cry with her on the drive home. I understand why she hates my God. It's not because her father and I speak one thing and live another. In that regard, I believe our daughter respects us and respects our faith; but still, she tells us she is atheist. It is easier for her not to believe in a God than to believe He exists and allows her to suffer years without end.

Why do the innocent suffer? It's an ancient question, one that is answered so much more easily in a theoretical doctrinal thesis than in real life, where actual, innocent, precious people are suffering. Where such depth of emotion as hers is involved, canned answers are not welcome.

Faith and Expectancy

My choice of Christian faith, faith that believes in the gifts of the Spirit as manifested in our day, in our time, only adds to my daughter's angst. It adds to her angst because I tout a God who is all-powerful, the same yesterday, today, and forever; a God who heals others while she is tortured by depression, volatility, anxiety, obsessions, and tics for most of her life. And with all of those challenges comes the battle of her identity and self-worth.

I admit, I have argued with God about my expectation for the miraculous and how my belief impacts my daughter. Would life have been better for her if my husband and I had taught her a lovely, neat gospel where God behaves only in a prescribed manner that is completely predictable, powerful in word only but seemingly not in deed? But in so doing, we would deny the reality of the Kingdom here and now, which includes the miraculous, as Jesus said it exists: "The kingdom of God has come upon you" (Matthew 12:28 NIV).

The coming of Christ is the advent of the Kingdom of Heaven as well, here now, and it includes the promise of a coming Kingdom. The Kingdom of God that is already here and yet to come is a paradox, one that leaves me both expectant and waiting. One that leaves my daughter confused and doubtful.

> The Kingdom of God that is already here and yet to come is a paradox, one that leaves me both expectant and waiting.

To cut expectancy out of the equation is to end up with a different summation. It's expectancy that arouses me out of the stupor of my sometimes lacking in positivity family dynamics to the needs of others around me. I know my God intervenes in the today, albeit not necessarily how I might dictate. And being Kingdom minded is not just looking forward to a coming Kingdom where God rules and reigns, tears are wiped away, and all suffering ceases. Being Kingdom minded also includes working with Him in establishing His Kingdom now, confident of His sometimes miraculous intervention.

Expectancy maintains hope for the now. Expectancy that includes experiencing God is what sustains me. I do not believe a less experiential Christian walk, founded on theological truth alone, could provide the strength and joy I find in relationship with my Father. Like the prophet Micah, I proclaim, "But as for me, I will watch expectantly for the LORD; I will wait for the God of my salvation. My God will hear me" (Micah 7:7 NASB).

In the meantime, my daughter waits for something more tangible—for relief. I actively research and provide every intervention available. And I provide for her the hope she needs until she discovers the Author of Hope for herself.

The Idol of the Ideal

I didn't realize I had expectations until those expectations were not realized. I was not the type of young woman who sat around writing out her imagined married name in cursive just to see how it looked. I didn't dream about wedding dresses or bouquets or dinner parties associated with a fictional wedding of the future. So when it actually was time for my wedding, I planned it with no pressures formed through years of longing.

The youngest of three, I had little exposure to babies and young children. My babysitting opportunities consisted mainly of filling in when my older sister was unavailable. At age eleven I landed my first babysitting job, watching three or four children only a few years younger than me. My sister gave up fifty cents an hour to me that night, and I felt honored to earn it.

I cannot remember ever holding a baby before my own. Three days after I gave birth to my first child, she was handed over to me to take home and raise, in spite of my profound ignorance. For anyone to say, especially me, that I had preconceived ideas of what I expected did not ring true. Yet over time, I discovered it was very true.

Before children, I was the kind of woman who believed in "plan the work and work the plan." When college professors said to read a chapter, memorize this information, or write an outline of that material, I did it. Predictably I earned A's, straight A's; and although I graduated with highest honors, I never attributed it to intelligence. I knew my classmates made different choices than I did when it came to self-discipline, so they earned B's or C's. If I did not study, I would fail. Cause and effect were well ingrained.

I thought it was as such with child raising. Parenting well (earning the grade), I thought, was largely the product of parental self-discipline, wise choices, and hard work. If I did it right, my children would turn out right.

Doing it right looked like modeling after my precious mother for some things and, like all offspring, doing it completely opposite for others. And doing it right meant aligning carefully with a whole host of other parenting axioms, some of which admittedly needed to be discovered in process. By doing it right, this parenting thing, my children would turn out just fine.

> Parenting well (earning the grade), I thought, was largely the product of parental self-discipline, wise choices, and hard work. If I did it right, my children would turn out right.

Normal ideals were assumed: ten fingers, ten toes, and typical neurology. My babies would be in Mom's Day Out one or two days a week for socialization and my own personal well balance. I would stay home with them when they were small children rather than pursue my former career outside the home. My marriage would be healthy. My children would attend public or private school according to their unique needs and the schools' offerings. They would have minor chores to do with checklists and behavior modification charts in order to learn responsibility. I would be active in their classrooms, building relationships with other moms, some I would secretly hope to influence to make their children a higher priority, to get the parenting thing "more right."

These ideals fueled grief when my children did not and could not march with the others in perfect formation. Yet I persevered with the ideals even in the face of the stark reality of a truth that was otherwise. My third grade daughter's difficulty transitioning (she screamed and raged) meant I was teaching commitment and responsibility to her by telling her, "I understand that you are doing something else right now. That is why I made sure you had transition warnings. You committed to children's choir, and we must go now. The choir needs every voice. Would you like to walk, or would you prefer to be carried?" It seemed she always chose to be carried, especially down hallways populated by other mothers with their compliant, neatly dressed wee ones. A chore list was light years beyond us.

I could go on for pages listing the ideals I never realized that were firmly established in my expectations. "No child of mine will ever be out of school and lying on my couch without a job and not going to college!" was just one of many that would have to topple. Before that ideal toppled, other ideals also toppled with multiple school placements, huge disparities between performance and IQ, suspensions, expulsions, and advocacy. Real life looked nothing like how it was supposed to look. In my cause-and-effect paradigm, humiliation didn't come just from those who were getting it "right," secretly hoping they could influence me to do it better; it was home grown.

Embracing the Real

I have learned to accept and embrace all three of my children for who they are: my firstborn with her typical neurology as well as my other two children with their brain chemistry differences. We share joys and sorrows together.

My husband and I have grown together as parents and partners through the challenges. We have cackled over the Christmas letters we could have written through the years.

The brain scans were a real boon! Who knew that the Prozac prescribed for all these years was helping our child's prefrontal cortex but wreaking havoc on the basal ganglia, another area in the brain? We have made real strides! We have been able to drop the antipsychotic too, and now our child is passing half of school classes this semester! Our daughter's discrimination lawsuit also is coming along nicely. One would think a corporation would know better than allowing a supervisor to openly mock an employee for tics. Our flexible spending account has been cut in half by the federal government. Now we get to use it up by January of next year rather than by April. Merry Christmas!

Our triumphs and challenges just don't read like those of the typical family. On good days, we laugh at the absurdities, the rage thrown over unloading a dishwasher, or the rage thrown over the pickle present on the cheeseburger. On less than good days, we feel the full brunt of the real or imagined judgmental stares our family attracts. We cry ourselves to sleep that night, unsure how to face another day.

It is the elevation of the ideal, unexamined respect for the ideal, that keeps us from laughing as we compare the behaviors and capabilities we expect of ourselves and of our children with our reality. In contrast, when we embrace the real, which goes beyond merely accepting our less-than-ideal family, we find and maintain the hope we need.

The elevation of the ideal can, if we let it, paralyze us to actions that are truly helpful and life-giving. But like roping the dictator statue in the town square and casting it into the street, we can dethrone the idol of the ideal.

Reflective Prayer

Heavenly Father,

I lay at Your feet the ideals that taunt me when my family situation does not measure up to what I expected. I choose to embrace what is my family and thank You for every member.

"Listen to my voice in the morning, LORD." Each day "I bring my requests to you" (Psalm 5:3), requests for the strength to reflect Your kindness, to set aside the ideals I've elevated, and to wait expectantly for You.

It's the expectancy that includes experiencing You that sustains me! Because of Your unfailing love, I can enter into Your presence. I worship You with deepest awe! "Lead me in the right path, O LORD," or my struggles will conquer me. "Make your way plain for me to follow" (Psalm 5:7–8).

So no matter what, I watch expectantly for You, Lord. I embrace the real as I wait for You, the God of my salvation. I decree as one who loves You that I will be filled with joy. You bless and surround me "with your shield of love" (Psalm 5:11-12). In Jesus' name I pray these words. Amen.

Chapter Three

Love Never Fails

He's perfect. Gloriously, wonderfully perfect. My 7-month-old grandson arrives from across the country with my eldest daughter and son-in-law to celebrate the holidays with my husband and me. He enthralls, mesmerizes me by his every move, his giggles, his attempts at crawling, his every glance.

I can see the purity, something so holy, so deep, in my daughter's eyes, the joy in her love for him. My son-in-law is well matched with my daughter. I see similar emotions in his father's eyes. This bundle they have brought into the world is the perfect culmination of the love they share.

There is nothing sinister, nothing unrighteous in the hopes, dreams, and expectations this couple shares for my grandson. We partake in this holy hope together, borne of love, the expression of love, the love that is described in 1 Corinthians 13:4–8 (NASB), "Love is patient, love is kind . . . love . . . does not seek its own . . . does not take into account a wrong suffered . . . rejoices with the truth; bears all things, believes all things, hopes all things, endures all things." In essence, "love never fails."

Childbirth itself is a testament to love. Out of the short-lived pain comes the beauty of a new life, so vulnerable, so valuable, so precious—a unique gift from God unlike any other ever born.

I still grapple with how an experience so pure, so holy, can morph into an idol of ideal when the future, for some couples, unfolds differently than anticipated. It is as though grief, another holy expression, is hijacked and taken to the wrong destination. It's a place of darkness, where some aspects of love may still be

> I still grapple with how an experience so pure, so holy, can morph into an idol of ideal when the future, for some couples, unfolds differently than anticipated.

present but endurance, belief, and hope in times of suffering and loss are absent. Good fruit comes out of love. Good fruit comes out of brokenness too, in spite of the pain. The pain you feel in unmet expectations has the potential to sow compassion and grace deep into your spirit. The pain your struggling child feels has the potential to sow dependence on God, resiliency, and compassion deep into that child's spirit. No good fruit, however, comes from idolatry.

The Promise of Hope

A promise was wrapped up in Abraham's child Isaac at his birth. God told Abraham, "I will establish my covenant with him as an everlasting covenant for his descendants after him" (Genesis 17:19 NIV). Sarah and Abraham had waited many years for that perfect culmination of their love. In this child lay promise unparalleled. Sarah and Abraham rejoiced in the truth spoken by God, believing all things and hoping all things. Their love for Isaac was pure, like my daughter and son-in-law's love for their son. Like my love for each of my children. And like the love you have for yours.

In Isaac's progeny lay the Hope for all of mankind (Genesis 22:18). Yet Abraham was instructed to lay Isaac on the altar, offering him back to God, the Giver of this gift. Abraham's first allegiance was to God, evidenced by his obedience to the mandate. But in his obedience, Abraham at no point in time sacrificed the truth of who Isaac was or stopped believing, stopped loving Isaac, stopped hoping.

Hebrews 11:17–19 says, "It was by faith that Abraham offered Isaac as a sacrifice when God was testing him. Abraham, who had received God's promises, was ready to sacrifice his only son, Isaac, even though God had told him, 'Isaac is the son through whom your descendants will be counted.' Abraham reasoned that if Isaac died, God was able to bring him back to life again."

For me to recognize and disavow the idol of the ideal in my own life is not to say I abandon my hopes, my dreams, or my joy in consideration of my children's present or future. It is not a cynical, "expect nothing and be grateful for anything I get" shift in perspective in order to guard my heart from the pain of disappointment. On the contrary, like Abraham, I lay down the ideal and hold fast to hope.

The Emptiness of the Idol

When Isaac's life was potentially taken away from Abraham, what did Abraham have left? Everything. "For the Scriptures tell us, 'Abraham believed God, and God counted him as righteous because of his faith'" (Romans 4:3). Faith, hope, and love remained, regardless of the circumstances.

When an idol of the ideal is established, the opposite occurs. Hope becomes wrapped up in the idol. When hope isn't there in the messy reality, all that's left is emptiness. It is as Judges 18:24 describes. When Micah's idols were stolen, he exclaimed, "What do you mean, 'What's the matter?' . . . You've taken away all the gods I have made, and my priest, and I have nothing left!"

Do you ever feel more like Micah than Abraham? Hope resting in expected ideals is an indicator something is amiss, an idol in the making.

Though Isaac's life as a young boy was spared, the inevitability of suffering and the good fruit that would come from it remained. Many years and several chapters later as recorded in Genesis, God led Isaac to Gerar, into a land of famine. Isaac had to live in that land and sow in that land of famine before he received the blessing of a hundredfold produce (Genesis 26:1–5, 12). Isaac, the promised one, had to hope and suffer as well.

We too must live in the "land" that has been allotted to us. As we "dig in," we trust God for the miracle of produce from a field we sometimes fear may be barren. We do everything we can with what we have, and we trust God for the outcome. Our hope is not dashed by ADHD rating scales, genetic testing, intelligence quotients, or lab test scores. Our hope is in God, His goodness, and His intentions toward us.

Good Gifts

Placing our hope in the ideal is wasted faith. Worse, the grief that's born of misplaced hope can block the joy God intends for us when we experience successes in our own household—even when they are different from those of a typical family.

> Placing our hope in the ideal is wasted faith. Worse, the grief that's born of misplaced hope can block the joy God intends for us.

When my daughter was young, I received a phone call one afternoon from her elementary school. The principal was elated to report to me "good news." My daughter had thrown rocks out on the playground, aiming at and hitting a boy's head. She then admitted her actions and willingly submitted to the daylong detention in the principal's office.

This news was incredible! It showed amazing progress! My daughter, who had struggled from an inability to understand cause and effect, behavior and consequences, just had a breakthrough. The principal understood my daughter, and she acknowledged the glorious day's news for what it was, in spite of the rock-throwing incident itself. I commended the principal for being so astute, and I reveled in the joy of that day!

If I had judged that occasion based on a standard of ideal, I would have missed the joy that was meant to be mine. After all, once again I had received a call from school, and once again my girl's behavior had created a problem. But on this occasion, my daughter had learned to connect the dots between behavior and consequences. The boon of this progress was far greater than the sting of blameworthiness. And unseen at the time, her learning that day was a milestone that would protect her from many potential mishaps in the future during her development as a young woman.

Joy motivates. It is said of Jesus that He "became obedient unto death" (Philippians 2:8 KJV), "for the joy set before Him endured the cross" (Hebrews 12:2 NASB). That joy was you and I, our redemption. We can follow Jesus' lead and allow joy to motivate us instead of allowing our joy to be stolen by the unholy urge to let our eyes drift toward what we don't have just yet. We can trust God for the outcome He has ahead and live in the land that has been given to us.

We love our children as is, of course. There is no question about our devotion or commitment. But it is not just the value of the child we need to grasp, which comes easily; it's the value of the task itself, of parenting children who are different from the ideal.

In the well-known parable of the talents in Matthew 25, all three stewards were given money in the form of coins called talents and assigned the task of managing the gift. The steward who received only one talent to manage buried it for two reasons. One talent compared to the five or ten talents given to the other stewards did not bear as great potential. Additionally, the steward buried the talent because he did not esteem his master (Matthew 25:24) enough to give the one talent his best efforts. This unholy perspective is supported in Luke's rendition of the story (Luke 19:12–14), which asserts that none of the subjects wanted the master to be king over them. I wonder what might have been the return had the steward who received one talent esteemed his master enough to give the task his best efforts?

The parable begs a comparison. If I focus on the academic, relational, and spiritual success of my friends' typical children, I might reasonably (although wrongly) conclude a lesser return is available for me. But unlike the stewards in the parable, I want the way I faithfully steward my parenting assignment to reflect my relationship to the loving Master. That relationship is not honored by actions merely to protect or bury my talent to keep it safe. I don't just love my child and excuse lack of forward momentum because of all the extra effort required to train. Instead I do everything possible to create the yield, and then I surrender the outcome to my loving Master.

Verse 15 of the Matthew 25 parable indicates disbursements were made to the stewards "according to their ability." Most people assume this verse means the steward who received one talent had the *least* ability (the verse does not say "least"). I think it is equally possible the steward had the *greatest* ability and was therefore given the greatest challenge.

It's the quality of my relationship with the Master, my belief in His good gifts and His intentions toward my children and me, not my ability, that aligns me with success. I plant in faith for a bountiful harvest from my parenting efforts. I have been given the opportunity to flourish under extenuating circumstances. And so have you.

> I plant in faith for a bountiful harvest from my parenting efforts. I have been given the opportunity to flourish under extenuating circumstances. And so have you.

The talent is the Giver's gift to give, and it's mine to steward well. The ability I have is from my relationship with the Most High. God empowers me to face a myriad of challenges far beyond my capacity, knowledge, or experience. It's the love of God for me that causes Him to turn my hardships into blessings, a hundredfold increase in a time of drought (Deuteronomy 23:5).

Isaac was given a barren field. Isaac's potential was tested, like the steward who received one talent, by being given less than others but with an equal expectation of yield. Although the gift of a child with hidden disabilities is not "less" in value or potential than that of a typical child, you may feel the impact of poor academic performance, lower achievement, and social inequities. But these challenges are not the yield. How will you steward what has been entrusted to you?

Support from All the Wrong Places

We parents know instinctively we must take care of ourselves if we are to excel in the care of our children, our families, and those relationships that matter most to us. The challenge is to find what we need in the right places.

Help is elusive within our barricaded cocoons of home. There, in the insulation of our private surroundings, we tend to be our own worst critics, painfully cognizant of our failings: the harsh words spoken, the misunderstandings, the guilt of watching those entrusted to us crash and burn. Thinking our way through our circumstances alone, at home, is not how we find the help we need.

Reading is one way to feed our spirits for self-care. But reading is also a solo activity. The temptation with reading is to withdraw into the confines of our own overwhelming experiences, failures, and even successes by going to our quiet place, safe place. And so we read and scour the Internet for some insight, some encouragement, and some camaraderie, even if only a digital connection. It is a lifeline.

The isolation from other human beings that happens as we read makes reading not the whole answer. Isolation leaves us with only our own resources mentally, emotionally, and spiritually. More is needed.

Another place we might go for help is outside us, to carefully chosen places where we think people will understand us. But to our dismay we find that many audiences aren't safe—at least they don't feel safe. They are filled with parents of typical children, couples and singles without children who don't have a clue, and critics of all parents, regardless of their challenges.

No one, not even I, could possibly understand everything you are going through, those times when you feel like you cannot tread water another moment without slipping beneath that demarcation between survival and drowning. Likewise, no one can truly understand the elation you feel over something that appears so trivial to others: food swallowed, a smile, a loving grasp for your hand from one that is crushingly tactile defensive or oppositional.

When my middle child with autistic spectrum type challenges was in elementary school, I squeezed a weekly prayer and women's study group into my evening schedule when my husband could cover for me. The women chatted about common parenting issues. I joined in when I could, careful not to disclose too much, too soon.

One evening I sat patiently, listening to how little Johnny wouldn't eat his beets or Suzie folded her clothes too messily. And then I shared the full weight of my burdens: the screaming rage attacks, the failed trial medication induced melt-downs, the risks of off-label use of medications, and the discomfort of well-meaning solutions offered by friends—almost always involving a pyramid marketed, prohibitively expensive product certain to cure all that ailed my daughter.

These women, I thought, had certainly heard me. They "got it." I had attended the group faithfully for over a year and was vulnerably transparent, embarrassingly so at times. That night and other nights I was so relieved to be heard and, I thought, understood.

One night sometime later in the year, I was running terribly late and had a choice to make: take my daughter home and miss group, or bring her with me. The women would want to meet my daughter, I reasoned, and to embrace this child I loved so desperately who at the same time caused me extreme distress.

We arrived with no commotion and slipped in almost unnoticed. The women were seated informally around the living room, some in chairs and many on the floor, as the leader and hostess taught. My child stayed very quiet but, because she is tactile seeking, went around the room and sweetly rubbed necks and shoulders. I was proud of her! She'd left her oppositional, demanding self at home. I was not embarrassed by her behavior in this group of women I had grown to value as my support, my intercessors, and my friends.

After the lesson, however, and in the hearing of several other women, the leader rebuked me sternly for the "horrific distraction" my child had been. I was astounded, appalled really, and a bit humiliated. Didn't she see how incredibly well my little girl had behaved? Hadn't she heard a single story I had shared over the past year? Didn't she understand how important this group, her leadership, had been to me?

If I had brought my child and she had raged, whined, acted out oppositionally, or took center stage while I watched on and ate bonbons, then I could understand. But she had been a delight. Any other child would have been welcome for one evening, I reasoned, so why wasn't mine? Bewildered and feeling betrayed, I left that evening tempted to withdraw into the solitude of my cocoon mislabeled as safe.

By the grace of God, a family counselor had spoken wisdom to me back in those early days when I was just learning how to cope. His words came ringing back to me. "You're looking for support in the wrong places. How could they possibly understand?" My counselor was right.

Life-Giving Voices

I could have gleaned many insights from a group like the one I attended. But only a select few people in my entire sphere of relationships could have heard the specifics of my daily struggles and been a life-giving voice to me. After this experience, I determined to seek out those select few, to not expect most others to fulfill that need in my life. Having only one or two who "got it," who understood, would really be okay. But where could I look if not in a group of Christian mothers?

At first I used the Internet. I made a key online friend who was walking a similar path. She understood, grieved, and rejoiced with me. Finding that first life-giving voice was like finding a four-leaf clover in a field.

I then began regularly calling an out-of-state friend. She was raising four adopted daughters who fit like stair steps in between the ages of her own three biological girls. The nature of my friend's expanded, non-typical family meant she would need to process emotional disorders, sexual abuse, brains damaged through the drug abuse of a biological mother, reactive attachment disorder, and later the children's own drug and alcohol abuse problems as well as incarcerations. I wanted to help and support her as much as I wanted her help and support.

When my friend and I poured our hearts out to one another, listening deeply without judging, I gained perspective on my life's challenges. She did as well, although I teased her that in order for her to gain perspective, she would need to call a Thai tsunami victim to find someone with life more difficult than hers! Just as God was filling me with grace, He was also filling her. I was a nonjudgmental sounding board who could laugh with her over the absurdities and remind her how awesome she was even though life was taking some unexpected turns. She gave the same to me and remains to this day a dear friend who truly understands how my life can be both tumultuous and glorious at the same time.

The truth is that God gives His grace to each one of us according to the specifics of our need. I look to Him directly and primarily for that grace and secondarily to the right sources He provides. I am fair and grace-giving to others who are raising typical children. How could those who are not raising children with hidden disabilities possibly understand my parenting challenges?

I have received life-giving words, unexpected provision, from God's compassionate, listening emissaries as well. Generalized human experiences, when shared with sensitivity, are bridges that minister to others. Struggling parents are less interested in hearing "It must be so hard for you! I don't know how you do it!" and more interested in lifelines such as, "I couldn't possibly understand the depths of what you experience on a day-to-day basis, but let me tell you how God showed up for me in my dark hour." I thanked God for those unexpected encouragements whenever they came.

When I was in Chennai, India, bringing encouragement to a friend who rescues trafficked women and children, I noticed that all the clovers in the grass nearby where I stood were four-leafed. I think of this insight in my times of need for camaraderie. When generalized conversations with others include who God is and how God intervenes, the life-giving voices I need are as easy to find as four-leafed clovers in Chennai.

Reflective Prayer

Heavenly Father,

I want You to rule over me as Master. I commit to You that I will steward my parenting assignment to the best of my ability, not seeing the assignment You have entrusted to me as less worthy of respect than the assignment You have given to another. You are in charge of disbursements! Stewardship is my charge. And best of all, outcome belongs to You. Remind me of these truths on days when my best efforts feel so pointless.

Thank You that my life is both tumultuous and glorious. I decree that Your grace is all I need. Your power works best in my weakness (2 Corinthians 12:9). I refuse to allow the ideal to steal my joy. Please bring voices that speak to me of Your sufficiency, including a few who truly understand the challenges I face. In Jesus' name I pray these words. Amen.

Chapter Four

The Battle

You hear them all the time.

You hear them when you lie awake at night, processing the events of the day. You hear them when you awaken in the morning, trying to decide how you can face the new day. You hear them as you drive to school or when you are interrupted at work to handle the latest crisis. You hear them as you drive to the counselor, the psychiatrist, and the specialists. You hear them as you walk down the hallway at church to drop your child off in Sunday morning class. There is nary a time you don't hear the enemy's lies, his spin on your life and circumstances.

The enemy's voice speaks lies to you, about you, about your parenting, about your child, about your child's future, about your family, and about what others are thinking. Those lies are a perpetual barrage of condemning, demoralizing, and undermining input, seemingly coming from deep within.

On other days, that lying voice is less active. During those times, you may be able to reach out and embrace the hope, the vision, and the path forward to a place better than today. On those days, you feel encouraged, even overwhelmed by the significance of your battle for the hearts and minds of your children, your beloved, precious children.

There legitimately is an enemy. Demonic involvement through injected, opposing voice is not just a philosophical consideration or a metaphorical personification of the concept of evil. It is truth. The enemy is real and powerful, a spiritual being against all you know is good and God. If you are familiar with the concept of spiritual warfare, you might recognize the leader of all evil and demonic forces by name: Satan, sometimes called the Devil, the Evil One, and the Father of Lies.

Ephesians 6:12 says, " For we are not fighting against flesh-and-blood enemies, but against evil rulers and authorities of the unseen world, against mighty powers in this dark world, and against evil spirits in the heavenly places." In 2 Corinthians 10:3–5 the apostle Paul admonishes us, saying, "For though we live in the world, we do not wage war as the world does. The weapons we fight with are not the weapons of the world. On the contrary, they have divine power to demolish strongholds. We demolish arguments and every pretension that sets itself up against the knowledge of God, and we take captive every thought to make it obedient to Christ" (NIV).

I've heard it said that what we need most is not to be taught, but to be reminded of what we already know. This I know: The enemy's goal in the battle against the family is to bring about broken and dysfunctional families, divorce, abandonment, risk to others (code for hurting or killing another), or risk to self (code for self-harm or suicide). In the first few skirmishes of the battle, the enemy's short-term goal is to rob you of hope, vision, and a path forward. The enemy's ultimate goal is continuation of the carnage into the next generations through emotional, spiritual, or even physical maiming.

Lies Versus Truth

The battle we face because of the enemy has two fronts: attacks from the enemy on the outside of us and attacks from the lies that have made a home within us. The attacks from the outside and from within are equally disabling.

Psalm 34:13 says to keep our tongues from speaking evil and our lips from telling lies. The apostle Peter says it is how we can enjoy life and see many happy days (1 Peter 3:10). I believe these words of truth are not talking about just refraining from telling lies to other people. That's Christianity 101. They also are about not telling ourselves the enemy's lies about us and our family members, about embracing those lies, and about speaking them as though they are truth.

Here is an example. An *antipsychotic* is a class of drug used for a variety of symptoms. The day my daughter was prescribed an antipsychotic for the first time, I was in shambles. I couldn't move past the root word, "psychotic." My daughter was not psychotic. It took me several days to fight the lie. I struggled against the thought that my little girl, so wonderfully loving with so much to offer, would never be considered "marriage material" for a quality young man because she needed and had taken an antipsychotic.

Inner lies like that one set themselves up against the knowledge we have received from God. Those lies call God a liar. Because they attack us from within, they can deceive us sometimes more easily than the enemy's more obvious outward attacks. Even worse, rather than fighting them, we are prone to protect the lies implanted in our spirits by saying we don't want to walk blindly or stupidly in denial. We reason wrongly that to believe something other than what we can plainly see is paramount to practicing a "name it and claim it," presumptuous faith that lacks credibility.

Truth, like lies, can be visible or invisible. Because we are human, the visible truth is so much easier to accept, even though we know we don't have to see with our own eyes the manifestation of something that is true in order for it to be true. Given the perspective of time, the seed I carry in my pocket is a mighty tree. Though the proposition may seem absurd in the moment, it is quite true. Likewise, the seed child suffering in this moment of her disability is a mighty tree that thrives and gives shade to others in their time of need.

> *My volatile child is headed for incarceration.*
> *Oppositional defiance precludes my child from ever surrendering his life to Christ.*
> *My mistakes define my parenting.*
> *I can't have a legitimate voice in the lives of others because my own home life is fraught with conflict.*
> *Outcome is dependent on my parenting, and I don't have what it takes.*

Have any of these lies attacked you from within, blinding you from the truth? These and other demoralizing, undermining thoughts about your family (you know your particulars all too well) are not in agreement with what God says, no matter how hopeless or bleak your circumstances seem day to day. In contrast, whatever God says is indeed true. "God's way is perfect! The promise of the LORD has proven to be true. He is a shield to all those who take refuge in him" (Psalm 18:30 GW).

The Scriptures are full of teachings that declare what is true about those who have committed their lives to Christ, about those who are thus righteous. What does God say specifically that is true about you? What does He say about your children?

Here's what He has said to me. "I have loved you with an everlasting love" (Jeremiah 31:3 NIV). "From everlasting to everlasting the LORD's love is with those who fear him, and his righteousness with their children's children" (Psalm 103:17 NIV).

What do the Scriptures say about our prayers? Matthew 6:6 says, "When you pray, go away by yourself, shut the door behind you, and pray to your Father in private. Then your Father, who sees everything, will reward you." This verse says to me that although I may feel at times like the heavens are impenetrable brass, my God assures me that I am not only heard but also will be rewarded for taking my petitions before Him.

Here's another lie you may have heard. Our difficult circumstances produce only suffering. I don't know about you, but I'm not a fan of suffering. Yet God says, "We can rejoice, too, when we run into problems and trials, for we know that they help us develop endurance" (Romans 5:3). In reality, the constancy of practice required to stay calm in the midst of my children's rages, to think in agreement with the Word of God while barraged with lies, and to walk in love through emotional assault produces a crop of Spirit fruit more difficult to obtain under easier circumstances.

No matter how oppositional my children, God's Word assures me that His grace immeasurably exceeds their sinful behaviors. I have no right to stand against His truth but only to affirm it. Romans 9:20 says, "Who are you, a mere human being, to argue with God? Should the thing that was created say to the one who created it, 'Why have you made me like this?'" My child's sinful self was crucified with Christ "so that sin might lose its power" in her life. She is not a slave to sin and neither am I (Romans 6:6). This fact is known through the truth of God's Word, not measured by checks on a behavior chart.

Be Nourished by Truth

Truth nourishes us. Lies dehydrate. To stand firm in the battle, I drink in as much as I can of the Living Water that provides me with the instructions and the empowerment for completing the task of parenting assigned to me by my loving Heavenly Father.

Truth nourishes us. Lies dehydrate.

Jesus explains this principle to His disciples, "My nourishment comes from doing the will of God, who sent me, and from finishing his work" (John 4:34). Since I am a follower of Christ, then likewise my purpose in life is to do God's will and work. I declare that I can walk honorably before God and achieve my purpose no matter how daunting my child raising challenges.

Romans 8:29 says, "For God knew his people in advance, and he chose them to become like his Son, so that his Son would be the firstborn among many brothers and sisters." Since He chose me before I was even born to be conformed to the image of Christ, I can rest assured God is actively empowering me in process, in the midst of every struggle. I can also rest assured that He chose my children to fulfill His purposes too.

Recently I met a woman who seventeen years ago had been in the front pages of national newspapers after being held hostage at gunpoint. For years afterward, she was incapacitated by post-traumatic stress disorder (PTSD) and has fought a valiant battle to get her life back. I encouraged her to blog from the safety of her home about her experiences, not so much about the trauma of the experience itself but the trauma of seeking help and the missteps of the uninformed that assume one can just "get over it."

She is a different person now than she was before, in more ways than the obvious. She offers compassion and a warm, demonstrative hug long before she ever offers counsel to others. She is devoid of condemning judgment. I marvel listening to her, and I see parallels between what she faced from well-meaning believers and what parents of children with hidden disabilities face. The trials of dealing with "detractors" who knowingly or unknowingly wound us are just as real as the actual parenting challenges themselves.

> The trials of dealing with "detractors" who knowingly or unknowingly wound us are just as real as the actual parenting challenges themselves.

Like my new friend, God has done a work in my heart, making me more like Him. And He is making you more like Him as well. You will not be the uninformed one who glares at the child with Down syndrome who is squealing with delight in the movie theatre. When you see a child behaving oppositionally in the grocery store, your first thought will not be in judgment of the mother. You may grieve over the mother's challenges, her lack of equipping and her hardships, or the child's inevitable pain managing himself, but judge self-righteously you will not. You are being actively transformed, conformed into the image of Christ, a bearer of His love and grace.

God's Word, infused deep into our spirits by the pain we face, empowers us. Best of all for me are those portions of Scripture that reveal the character of God.

Psalm 25:8 says it is because God is good that He instructs mankind, not because mankind is good. "Good and upright is the LORD; therefore he instructs sinners in his ways" (NIV). That is an important truth for me to recall when I am feeling like an utter failure and am praying for strategy on how to tackle a parenting issue. I can count on God's goodness, drink in His nourishment, and expect instruction to be forthcoming—so that I, like Jesus, can do the will of God.

Choose Your Weapon

Much truth has been written about positive thinking and its power to change the way we act. Even so, the power of positive thinking is a watered down weapon of warfare against Satan, a dull sword in a combatant's hands against a lethal enemy who will stop at nothing less than your annihilation. Your greatest spiritual weapon of offense is not positive thinking but the Sword of the Spirit, the Word of God (Ephesians 6:17). With it in your mind and heart, as well as on your lips, you are able to stand firm when the enemy on the outside or the lies within attack.

At times I feel isolated and cut off from God's restorative presence. When these times come, I combat the lie of helplessness with the sword of truth, which says I am the temple of God whose Spirit lives in me twenty-four hours a day, seven days a week, regardless of circumstances (1 Corinthians 3:16). When I am attacked with the lie that today's failures make me particularly odious to God, my sword strikes back with the sharp-edged declaration that my life is "a Christ-like fragrance rising up to God" (2 Corinthians 2:15).

You see, time spent reading and meditating on the Word of God is not merely a spiritual discipline or one more brick to add to your trudging load, another area where you can fall under its weight. Instead, consuming the Word provides nourishing truth and life to your innermost being, life that defeats the lies of the enemy.

Nonfulfillment of any chosen discipline, spiritual or otherwise, can add negligence to your perceived list of personal deficiencies. Unfortunately, a well-populated index of shortfalls feeds the root of unhealthy self-loathing, which grows to encompass more than just parental failures. So understanding that drinking deeply of the truth of God's Word as your instruction and empowerment, not just as your spiritual obligation, frees you to enjoy its refreshment without self-condemnation.

Grab Times with God

Transparency about the facts never contradicts God's truth. It's the interpretations of facts, the conclusions, which are suspect. "My child screamed for forty-five minutes today" may be a fact, but "I can't handle this" and "Life sucks and then you die," and "I'm completely ill-equipped!" are erroneous and defeating lies that fly out of our mouths, defended by our determination to be "real." Life is hard, very hard for you right now. That is truth. But also true is that God can give you grace, buoying you in situations that would have sunk anyone else. Your times with God provide the input you need to combat the lies.

I love my early morning time with God, but here's what happened one morning when I missed it. My husband and I had guests the previous night. The teen of a family in transition that had lived with us for several months asked if he and his family could please join us for decorating our Christmas tree and driving around to see lights. The family, whom we had grown to love deeply, was gloriously stable at the time, but holiday traditions were a void in their lives. This teen remembered ours fondly. So we made it happen for him and his family on a night that they could join us. It was a long night, and we went to bed late.

I didn't experience guilt the next morning, only disappointment from missing my early worship. I had "stood up" my Best Friend. We shared that disappointment, but we both understood. The trade-off of the night before was an expression of my relationship with Him and the love that He gives us for others.

Not grabbing times with God happens. But if I skip too often, I just have to regroup and evaluate the trades I've been making to ensure they have been righteous ones. And I have to make other adjustments in my day so time with God is not shortchanged too much or too often. To be completely honest, sometimes at night I'm unwinding on social networking, not watching my time, or allowing social acceptableness to dictate when I leave an event. At the time I hardly realize what I'm trading until the next day, when I awaken late and miss my morning time with God. The loss, the unpreparedness for battle as a result, weakens me for the day ahead.

I have learned to be creative in grabbing Scripture and worship time with my Savior whenever and wherever. When my kids were younger, I would often have one earbud in to listen to worship music while the other ear was open to what was happening around me. It helped keep me focused. When driving, I sometimes even used noise-canceling headphones. I explained to my children that mommy wasn't ignoring them, but that she wouldn't be able to hear them well when the headphones were on. I could actually hear them some, but this action discouraged interaction without being rude to them.

Those headphones were an awesome investment. I have had far more near collisions from being distracted by fighting siblings or children demanding my attention than I ever have had from hearing impairment through headphones. Another great investment was my audio Bible, obtained online and downloaded onto my smartphone. In settings of few interruptions, I was able to listen to Scripture and enjoy some equipping time. When it was too difficult to sit down for an hour and read the Word, when the weeds needed pulling or the dishes needed washing, listening to audio Scripture was a way to kill two birds with one stone and become entrenched in the Word. This was a powerful discovery for me.

Although audiobooks were perfect for house cleaning, yard work, and extended drives, I found my mind wandered when listening to reading of book text alone, devoid of engaging sound effects. I am more visually attuned than auditory, so purchasing a high quality, dramatized audio Bible was key for my ability to focus.

Recognize the lies you have embraced about the impracticality of spending intimacy-fostering time with God. Arm yourself to maintain hope before, during, and after each skirmish in the battle, a function of alignment with the veracity of Heaven. Grab the times you need, and make the most of them in whatever ways work best for you.

Declare the Truth

Scouring the Word is a way to gather truth that can be spoken definitively over your life circumstances. It equips you to make declarations, or proclamations on your circumstances, by speaking what God says is true.

"Understand, therefore, that the LORD your God is indeed God. He is the faithful God who keeps his covenant for a thousand generations and lavishes his unfailing love on those who love him and obey his commands" (Deuteronomy 7:9). That verse becomes to me, "Father, I understand that You indeed are God! You are faithful and keep Your promises to the generations that come after me, including my own children. I love You and obey Your commands. So I can count on You lavishing Your love on me and on my family!" Or, when I am feeling particularly aggressive in my spirit, it sounds more like the following spoken directly over the affront: "I declare You are faithful! You keep Your promises to my children! By the blood of Jesus, I decree we receive Your love lavished over each one of us!"

Such declarations serve as a reminder to your spirit as well as to the demonic spirits that aspire to confuse you with lies. Declarations and decrees are a prayer strategy that aligns your life with truth. Collecting declarations that are in direct contrast to the lies you combat daily can be compared to what happens in those role-playing video games: you amass obscured weapons, one after another, as you bound your way through the battle unfolding before you.

My children love video games. The player controls the moves of a leading character, who is immersed in a complex story line requiring battles with enemies, called bosses. Victories over the bosses progress the contender to higher and higher levels of play. Different strategies are required to confront each boss in a video game. Strategies typically involve weapons obtained during maneuvering through the fictional world to defeat the boss.

Watching my children play these games has given me insight into my own life strategies for victory. Each lie that assaults my mind and spirit needs a specific counterattack. The declarations of truth I have amassed are ready weapons to grasp for the next skirmish. It is no longer self-discipline that motivates me to immerse myself in God's Word. It's the reality of the battle ahead and my very real need to prepare for it in advance.

I don't mean to trivialize real life by the gaming analogy, but God has a way of speaking through the simplest things. It is not just self-discipline that motivates video-gaming children to check behind every bush and in every chest for "jewels" (rewards) or "weapons" (implements) to further them along in their electronic game. They know through experience that they will "die" and have to "re-live" that portion of the game repetitively until they can obtain and use the right strategy against each and every foe they encounter.

Children get really good at these games because they begin to uncover patterns and predict accurately. We can get really good with our battle strategies too. We can discern what's ahead and arm ourselves with declarations of truth in advance. Our stakes are much higher than theirs in a fictional game. We are fighting for our very lives and for the lives of our children.

Brandish the truth you already own. Seek out the provision awaiting discovery. Shift your thinking to recognize the lies. Battle with counter-prayers. Advance from "peasantry" petitioning prayers that beg from the Lord of the Manor to declarations, proclamations, and decrees of a noble who is counting on the authority of the King.

Reflective Prayer

Heavenly Father,

Align my thinking with Yours. When I search Your Word, highlight for me what You have definitively said to be true about me and about my children.

You will grant me Your blessing when I do what You have called me to do. I long to keep my lips from repeating the lies fed to me by the evil one of this world that is committed to my failure, and I want to "enjoy life and see many happy days" (1 Peter 3:9–10). "Set a guard, O LORD, over my mouth; Keep watch over the door of my lips" (Psalm 141:3 NASB).

In agreement with Your Word, I decree that Your love is with me "from everlasting to everlasting" and Your righteousness is with my children's children (Psalm 103:17 NIV). I declare that the promises of the Lord will continue to prove true in my life and in the lives of my children (Psalm 18:30). In Jesus' name I pray these words. Amen.

Chapter Five

Unrighteous Trades

My friend in Indonesia tells me many who identify themselves as Christians still seek out the services of witch doctors for healing or prosperity. Although a small fee such as a chicken is involved, the greater cost for such services is unseen. A behind-the-scenes, unrighteous trade happens in the spirit realm, often leading the seeker to become impoverished financially and crippled spiritually. Some who wrongly seek aid from witch doctors experience lives rife with seemingly inexplicable losses and even death.

This sad story is not the first time I have heard of unrighteous trades, but it reminds me of the words in Ezekiel 28:18 (NASB), considered by many an allusion to Satan. "By the multitude of your iniquities, in the unrighteousness of your trade you profaned your sanctuaries." Dealing with a demonically em-powered witch doctor in order to create ideal circumstances for oneself or family certainly is not a fair trade. And most unrighteous trades are not so overtly spiritual or obviously detrimental. Yet the scenario of an unrighteous trade is common. In order to get what is wanted, the ideal, the person trades something far more precious, aware of it or not.

> The scenario of an unrighteous trade is common. In order to get what is wanted, the ideal, the person trades something far more precious, aware of it or not.

For parents of children with hidden disabilities, insistence on the ideal can wreak havoc. They may not go to witch doctors, but the refusal to accept the reality of their circumstances can cause unwise decisions regarding the family and, in the process, trade away something more valuable. Internal visions of the ideal are what keep many mothers or fathers from considering diagnoses, medications, and counseling for their children. It is not ideal to have a child with a hidden disability; however, it is even less ideal to block a child from intervention or treatment that is desperately needed.

Head in the Sand

When my head is in the sand, refusing to acknowledge my child's differences, I am unable to open my mouth and speak life to my child, fostering his self-acceptance and empowering him to take ownership and responsibility for his behaviors. I am also not able to seek the relief my child needs to help make the playing field with that of his peers as close to equal as possible.

Once when my 8-year-old son attended Sunday school at our mega church, he made a delightful new friend. The boy was homeschooled, disturbing no one with his obvious tics. I took this child as a guest of my son to a restaurant with an expansive indoor playground and observed his struggle to transition between tasks, distractibility, hyperactivity, and obsessiveness. I tested the waters by casually mentioning to him that his playmate, my son, had Tourette's syndrome, the reason he had certain unusual (identical) behaviors. No lights went on in the child, so I stopped and watched the two boys continue to play.

When I took the boy home, I decided it just might be the time to have a careful chat with his mom. I'm no doctor and don't diagnose, but certain symptoms are profoundly evident to the experienced eye. The mom's response? Very little. She was perfectly attentive to her son in every other way yet disinterested in the possibility that something might be wrong.

Here are the words I longed to speak to her son:

> *I see the shame on your face when you turn away to try to hide your tics. In spite of what you might think sometimes, you're not crazy. You are not doing those things because you want to. There's a spot in your brain that sends you those behavior signals. It's not a big deal. It's just brain chemistry. That's all it is.*
>
> *Your brain chemistry is also why you struggle to transition from one task to another, why you lose the battle to sit still even though you try so hard. If it bothers you so much that you want to explore treatments, let your mom know. In the meantime, I understand how hard it is for you, and I give you full credit for all of your efforts to manage it as well as for your successes. I see your heart, even though from others, in other settings, you may endure harsh corrections. Please just know: I am on your side.*

Those words were never spoken. I have no idea if the child ever got help. And I don't know if his parents ever faced the reality that their child likely had a neurological condition that fueled social rejection, academic hardship, and personal failure.

I believe it is an unrighteous trade when parents shy away from the pain of diagnosis, possible stigma, and shame (albeit unwarranted). By doing so, they allow the full brunt of the hidden disability, without navigational aid, to impact their struggling children. The parents keep their "ideal" world, but at what cost?

When parents choose to ignore their children's need for help, they keep their parenting ideals, their prejudices against medicating children, and their judgments against diagnoses that can't be measured through a blood test. They appear unscathed as extended family, peers, and siblings further ostracize their "nightmare child." But their choice not to act requires their children to bear rejection by others as the children's personal responsibility.

Which Path Forward?

Why should the ideal dictate the path forward?

I always said I would never have an adult child of mine sitting on my couch, eating my food, unemployed, and not in school. That was the ideal. Yet I had that scenario in my home. I had to discard my ideal and look at reality for what it was.

Why should the ideal dictate the path forward?

As a young adult, my daughter did not have the mental health to be a student or to work outside of the home. Sending her out to live on her own at some ideal age in my mind would have booted her toward homelessness, sexual exploitation, and untold suffering. Those outcomes were far out of proportion to my objections over the inappropriateness of her actions based on her numerical age.

Honest assessment of the situation resulted in an understanding that my daughter needed to be at home. In spite of her high IQ, she needed her home bedroom for a few more years before she was ready for further education, employment, or even job training. This reality certainly was not ideal, but it was real.

My decision to allow my daughter to remain at home for several years in her adulthood was difficult to explain to extended family eager to cheer her on and launch her into her own life. But regardless of their kind protestations, I knew keeping her home for some time was right. My conscious decision to abandon the ideal made hosting her into her twenties more of a joy for me than the false shame society inflicted.

To this day my daughter remains a delight to my heart. I shudder now at the cost of an unrighteous trade I could have made in order to honor an idol of ideal.

I believe the ideal is what drives the knife in deeper, causing personal pain, when children of others behave beautifully in public and achieve goals that are typical for their age. A report card beyond elementary school not peppered with F's is in reality a sight to behold in my household, but the ideal makes me think it should be otherwise. Whenever the ideal becomes my expectation, the "less than" experience in my family can fuel anger, pain, and bitterness. Better the pain I experience be pure, uncontaminated by destructive comparisons.

A far better place for my grief emotion is on the reality of my daughter, who experiences social rejection, debilitating depression, and humiliations. Also on the reality of my high school aged son, who is passionate about architecture yet hasn't passed a math class in three years. And I grieve and yes hate equally the suffering all of us endure together as a family with children who have hidden disabilities.

Facing Suffering

In spite of my disdain for suffering, I'm cognizant that Christ learned obedience through suffering. Hebrews 5:8 plainly states, "Even though Jesus was God's Son, he learned obedience from the things he suffered." Suffering brings benefit, even to the Son of God. That Jesus needed to learn obedience is difficult to grasp. If suffering is a learning experience and becomes a benefit to the One who is sinless, how much more so can suffering become a benefit to me or my children, since all of us were born into sin and struggle against our flesh?

There is a proper response to suffering. It's not rolling over and saying, "More, Lord!" Nor is a proper response denial. It's facing it head on, with honest, appropriately placed emotion.

I think many Christians unconsciously visualize Christ in prayer on the Mount of Olives prior to His betrayal like some of the artists' renditions: Jesus kneeling, gazing into heaven with a pious look on His face, calmly proclaiming, "Not My will but Thine." But that picture is not Jesus' reality. Hebrews 5:7 (NIV) says, "During the days of Jesus' life on earth, he offered up prayers and petitions *with fervent cries and tears* (emphasis mine) to the one who could save him from death and he was heard because of his reverent submission."

At times Christians act as though reluctant acceptance of affliction without protest is synonymous with trusting God, somehow more spiritual than openly sobbing. If not to acknowledge suffering and remain completely quiet about it is God's perfect model, I believe Jesus in prayer that day would have merely envisioned His upcoming march into death without an intercessory peep! The reality is that Christ felt the full brunt of His impending sentence, in spite of complete trust in the Father. The truth is that Christ knew no sin, yet in Gethsemane He addressed His Father over His circumstances "with fervent cries and tears, to the one who could save him from death." It's the idol of the ideal that causes us to envision Jesus otherwise.

The Bible relates how the Israelites suffered as they maneuvered through the desert on their way to the Promised Land. We expect Jesus' response to suffering to differ from the stiff-necked Israelites, and it did in many ways, but we easily can miss the commonalities between those responses.

Jesus faced His suffering. He didn't enjoy it. He didn't deny it. He wanted to escape it. Jesus knew only the Father could save Him from death and the suffering it entailed: physical, emotional, and spiritual suffering as He bore the sins of the world. The Israelites also legitimately suffered. Dying of dehydration out in the hot sun, wandering year after year in the desert, going without the relative plenty back in Egypt: these were not enjoyable or escapable.

It is easy to discount the Israelites' complaint about monotony of diet and lack of meat. After all, many people these days choose to be vegetarian, and large portions of the global population subsist on rice. But lack of water is most definitely a legitimate concern. Because I live in arid Colorado, water on extended hikes through the Rocky Mountains is of utmost priority. Similarly, to underestimate one's need for water is one of the quickest ways to die next to stepping off the edge of a cliff in the Grand Canyon.

Neither Jesus nor the Israelites were in denial about their suffering or circumstances. Both acknowledged and verbalized their situations. Both fully entered into the emotional impact of what they faced. And both knew the Father could change the situation and outcomes. But these details are where the similarities between Jesus' response to suffering and Israel's response end.

The Israelites did not bring their hardships to the Lord. Rather, they complained to others in the hearing of the Lord (Numbers 11:1). They wailed to each other (Numbers 11:4–6). And they especially wailed to Moses (Numbers 11:13), increasing his burden. When the Israelites came to the bitter waters of Marah, they murmured against Moses (Exodus 15) rather than cry before God as the One who carried them on eagles' wings and brought them to Himself (Exodus 19:4). They cried against God. They did not come *to* God as His treasured possession (Exodus 19:5).

Jesus came *to* His Father in reverent submission. Jesus also prayed that we too might know the love of the Father just as He knew His Father's love (John 17:23). In contrast, the Israelites did not trust God. Instead they blamed God. They failed to see the difference between acknowledging the realities of their situation and assigning blame. The Israelites blamed God, accused God, and stood in agreement with the enemy, the father of lies.

Choosing Jesus' Way

When we observe the similarities and the differences between how Jesus responded to suffering and how the Israelites responded, we can make application to our own lives. Who hears first about what happened behind closed doors in your home—others or God alone? Do you go to your Father as an afterthought, using the people in your life as your real emotional support? It's a far better choice to acknowledge our need and shift our search for emotional support to Father God and then secondarily allow God to use friends, family, and caring professionals to come along beside us.

> It's a far better choice to acknowledge our need and shift our search for emotional support to Father God and then secondarily allow God to use friends, family, and caring professionals to come along beside us.

Or maybe we are like those who don't say anything, ever, to anyone, and just suffer through our children's rages and the carnage on the family. We fear being like the Israelites in the wilderness, who complained about the monotony of their diets and their lack of fresh water. We unconsciously equate their sin with noticing and acknowledging their lack. We imagine they should have been (and we ought to be) more like the apostle Paul's assertion, to be content in whatever state (Philippians 4:11).

Job is probably the most famous sufferer in the Bible. His lament was loud and long, as were his prayers for help. After he endured his grievous losses and suffering, it was said of Job, "Through all this Job did not sin nor did he blame God" (Job 1:22 NASB).

I know my Father does not require or expect me to walk in denial and feigned acceptance of the difficult situations I face in my life or the grieving I endure over my children. I know it is not more spiritual to pretend that the pain I face daily is bearable or somehow defensible. Do you?

Scripture tells us Jesus did not sin. Therefore, fully acknowledging His suffering, not liking His suffering to the point of desiring escape, verbalization, crying out, and tears over His situation was not, is not, and will never be counted sin, failure, or weakness.

Just in case you missed my last point, let me reiterate that

- full acknowledgment of suffering,
- not liking suffering to the point of desiring escape,
- verbalizing,
- crying out, and
- tears

do not equal

- sin,
- failure, or
- weakness on your part

because Jesus did these same things, and they are *not* sin for Him or us.

Is it possible we hold ourselves to an unreasonable standard and then condemn ourselves for falling short of what Christ was not even expected to do? Do we require more out of ourselves in this respect than the Father required out of His own Son? If so, it's no wonder we struggle with demoralization alongside the hardship! That unreasonable standard we inflict upon ourselves too is an idol of ideal.

> Is it possible we hold ourselves to an unreasonable standard and then condemn ourselves for falling short of what Christ was not even expected to do?

Sometimes when people cry out before God, immediate relief comes. When Moses cried out to God, God miraculously provided manna and water. He also provided a strategy for dealing with the overwhelming responsibilities of leadership. I believe God is miraculously able to reach down and touch every situation that brings pain in my life. Just like Shadrach, Meshach, and Abednego who were thrown into the fiery furnace by Nebuchadnezzar, I too expect intervention and deliverance (Daniel 3:16–18). But even if God does not deliver when and how I request, may it be known that I will never stand in agreement with the enemy in accusation against my God.

Jesus, the very Son of God, was not delivered from enduring the cross. Jesus had to walk through the darkest valley, motivated by the joy set before Him. That joy couldn't have been just His position with the Father or the glory that awaited Him. Jesus had those benefits prior to coming to the earth to live and die. The joy set before Jesus was us, our salvation. We were what made His suffering worthwhile. Jesus demonstrated for us the loving character of our God, the character that creates in us the trust to submit to His will in the middle of our loud cries and tears.

The psalmist declared, "Even when I walk through the darkest valley, I will not be afraid, for you are close beside me. Your rod and your staff protect and comfort me" (Psalm 23:4). Like the psalmist, like Jesus, we are free to fully acknowledge the reality of those things in our lives that bring pain and suffering. It is not sin, weakness, or failure to verbalize, to desire escape, or to cry out before our God. Knowledge of His loving character guards our hearts from accusations against Him. Crying out to God whenever we need to and especially in the middle of our circumstances is healthy and the way that we walk out our faith. Even through the valley of the shadow of death, He is with us (Psalm 23:4).

Intercession

We can face suffering without denial or minimalizing the reality of our circumstances. We can look to God and affirm the psalmist's declaration, "You keep track of all my sorrows. You have collected all my tears in your bottle. You have recorded each one in your book" (Psalm 56:8). And we can cry out to God as the One who carries us on eagles' wings and brings us to Himself. Those cries are intercession.

Intercession is a godly way to process through your suffering. It brings Jesus close beside you. Like God intervened for Moses by providing strategy, intervened for Daniel's friends thrown into the furnace by rescuing them outright, and intervened for Jesus by enabling Him to obey His Father's will and making every bit of suffering worthwhile, God intervenes for you. You can add to your tears and cries of intercession, using in prayer all you know of God's will expressed in His Word to address what is wrong in your family. And you can stand in His authority, realigning your reality.

Reflective Prayer

Heavenly Father,

Here I am before You with loud cries and tears.

I'm acknowledging the lack in my life; I'm acknowledging too my fears, my disappointments, my failures, the judgments made against me, the judgments made against my child, and yes, the judgments I've made against myself. Even "when I walk through the darkest valley . . . you are close beside me. . . . [You] protect and comfort me" (Psalm 23:4). "You keep track of all my sorrows. You have collected all my tears in your bottle. You have recorded each one in your book" (Psalm 56:8).

I address You with loud cries and tears, and I see You here, holding Your arms out to me. I melt in reverent submission. I snuggle deeply in Your arms, "like a weaned child rests against his mother," composed and now quieted (Psalm 131:2 NASB).

I rest in the authority of Your Word. Jesus has left me "peace of mind and heart," the kind of all encompassing peace that I cannot get from any other source (John 14:27). I speak this reality into my life now. In Jesus' name I pray these words. Amen.

Chapter Six

Seeking Help

One question I am asked perhaps more than any other is simply, "When should we seek help?"

Two of my children have Tourette's syndrome, and I have sought help for both of them. Yet I have read that many children have Tourette's syndrome and are never even diagnosed. The mild motor or vocal tics are considered nothing more than an idiosyncrasy. I have heard too of adults discovering their childhood challenges are attributable to autistic spectrum characteristics that were never identified. Also, I have learned that when mild, the behavioral and academic difficulties of attention deficit hyperactivity disorder (ADHD) are deemed manageable for some through diet, exercise, and structure—customized interventions any child might benefit from.

Given these and other variables, the key question to ask when considering when to seek help is this: "Does this 'difference' I observe (potentially a brain functioning one) interfere with living in ways that significantly impact my child's present and potential for the future?" If the answer to that question is no, then intervention is probably not necessary, even if technically a child may have an identifiable diagnosis.

Several conditions, such as high-functioning autism, are no longer even seen as a disability by some who have autism, by their parents, and by autism activists. Instead, autism is considered just a difference, evidence of a diverse populace. I lean toward that grace-filled view of diversity. I have come to this understanding in part because my daughter has taught me to think in terms of "other abled" rather than disabled. Focusing on what a child *can do* rather than on what a child *cannot do* is a healthy approach.

Unfortunately, many children with hidden disabilities are indeed either somewhat disabled or at least hindered with symptoms that interfere substantially with life. My daughter, for example, has a very loud screaming tic. We've learned that tics can come and go, but currently her life is filled with the humiliation and stress of being a beautiful young woman who screams without warning.

These outbursts give others a corrupted impression of her sanity. More important, her anxiety levels soar whenever she attempts to leave the house, trapping her at home with her dreams of achievement and visions of success. I see her crumpled frame sobbing by her bedroom door and grieve with her. Withholding treatment from her, I believe, would be cruel. So I do what I can to help her, to seek the interventions that free her to live a better life.

My husband and I began seeking help for our daughter when she was three. Her volatility was interfering with the acquisition of age-appropriate motor skills even as her intellect soared. Additionally, we could not potty train her. Her symptoms even at that young age, we concluded, were interfering significantly with her ability to live her life.

As young parents from immediate families not exhibiting marked brain chemistry challenges, we missed the overt signs that should have screamed obsessive-compulsive disorder (OCD) and sensory integration disorder (also known as sensory processing disorder or SPD). But what we could identify very clearly was that this child was struggling and suffering. Her suffering alone was enough for us to seek help.

The Right Professionals

To whom does one go for professional help when a child has developmental problems? A pediatrician? The following experience was our introduction to the world of medical intervention.

The first general pediatrician we consulted considered himself capable of diagnosing and treating brain chemistry, although to my knowledge he never pursued any additional training in child psychiatry. He prescribed my preschooler Adderall for ADHD symptoms. On this medication, in the middle of a family vacation, she body slammed a plate glass window in a fit of rage because she could not choose between two pencils in a gift shop. Although her behavior seemed severe, we were accustomed to her rages, so we didn't immediately become too alarmed.

On another day during that same summer vacation, we observed something characteristically different. She sustained a five-hour tantrum (much to the amusement of the guards) on the floor of the Air and Space Museum in Washington, DC, while I tended to her, trying to calm her. Meanwhile, the rest of my family enjoyed the tour without us. It was then that I knew something more must be done.

At a loss over how to intervene, I called the pediatrician right there from the museum during the tantrum. My call to report the extreme behaviors yielded instructions simply to double her medication. I was horrified by that response. Although appropriately polite, I fired him instead. When we returned home, I sought help through other avenues.

Lesson learned: After you make that first step to seek help from a professional, follow it with one just as important. Trust your instincts as a parent rather than just assume the doctor, any doctor for that matter, knows best. The counsel I received across the airwaves to "double her medication" was my wake-up call to that reality.

After you make that first step to seek help from a professional, follow it with one just as important. Trust your instincts as a parent rather than just assume the doctor, any doctor for that matter, knows best.

A year later, I heard that pediatrician I fired had abandoned his wife, children, and medical practice to run off with a Russian pen pal. The detail may seem irrelevant, but I'm making a point about the fact that MD does not spell G-O-D.

Let me be clear. Obviously, this doctor's indiscretions and moral failures were unrelated to the care my daughter received, either the excellent care for routine childhood illnesses or the inadequate care she received for her hidden disabilities. But doctors are beset by the same frailties as all of mankind. They are susceptible to over reaching their skill or specialization level, with all good intention. As a parent, I must carefully discern between a doctor's desire to treat my child and the actual expertise required to diagnose and intervene. Physicians have limitations and even weaknesses, in spite of every doctor's impressive intellectual fortitude that leaves the general public in awe.

Once you determine the need for help, be tenacious in getting what you need. Subtle, long-term mismanagement can cost you dearly, so understand the role of general pediatricians trained to see a wide range of children for a wide range of issues. Wise pediatricians who do recognize a brain chemistry issue can give you a referral to a child psychiatrist. If the first referral does not yield good results, continue your search for help. It is unwise to confuse any physician's stellar bedside manner for competence; pleasantries and prescriptions are no substitute for the academics of specialization.

After the sad episode with that first pediatrician, at a loss and still completely ignorant, my husband and I began to devour literature on ADHD, the disorder mentioned by the discharged pediatrician. Our wonderfully brilliant child could barely function, hindered by a fuse significantly shorter than an average child in addition to incontinence and sensory sensitivities. We, and especially she, needed help. Doing our homework, educating ourselves to find the right professionals, was our next step to find help.

Psychologists and Psychiatrists

Late that same summer, when my daughter was tested for kindergarten readiness by our chosen prospective elementary school, I was told by school officials that my precious baby, already reading fluently and casually doing division in her head, had cried, disengaged, and curled up in a ball, "acting autistic." Rather than gain admittance into the private school of our choice, she received a referral to a mental health professional. Without a clean bill of health, we were told, our child was unwelcome in a school ill-equipped to teach children with special needs.

The school official requiring documentation of typical neurology provided the name of a local psychologist. A psychologist is a doctoral level specialist who studies behavior. A psychologist is a PhD (Doctor of Philosophy) or PsyD (Doctor of Psychology) in clinical or counseling psychology. Some are specialists in treating children. In retrospect, a more appropriate referral might have been to a child psychiatrist, a medical doctor (MD) with specialized training in psychiatry as it relates to children. At the time, we did not understand the difference between the two.

The roles and specialties of medical professionals can be confusing to the uninitiated. A psychiatrist is a medical doctor who specializes in studying the brain and its functions. In addition to undergraduate education and then medical school and licensure, child psychiatrists have four years in psychiatry residency and an additional two years of subspecialty training and supervision in child psychiatry before being released to practice.

Psychiatrists address both the biology of the brain and the social implications that are part and parcel. These medical specialists are deeply knowledgeable about neurological conditions, typical development, and appropriate interventions that include medications and their effects. Their knowledge goes significantly beyond that of a pediatrician and in areas different than that of a psychologist.

Since we were referred to a psychologist, we began there. My daughter's first psychologist was Jewish, which was ironic considering what happened next. She chose to draw for him the Christian plan of salvation with Satan basking in the burning flames of hell, complete with the cross of Christ bridging the gap between Earth and God's throne in heaven, illustrating the substitutionary redemptive death of the Messiah. The psychologist asked us how long we had been sexually molesting her. Not a very positive first visit.

We were not devastated; we were rightly outraged. But since we needed expert analysis and a report to give to the school officials, we concealed our offense. The psychologist had not attempted to get to know us to determine our character prior to making his serious and unfounded accusation. Instead, he proceeded with his line of questioning and more pronouncements.

He concluded, through one visit, that the structure my husband and I had put in place after reading about ADHD was actually the causative agent for our daughter's maladies. His prescription was for us to relax the structure in our daughter's routine. Fortunately for our reputations, "parental rigidity" was all he wrote up in his diagnostic report, and our daughter received the coveted kindergarten admission "clean bill of health." Life ahead would prove differently.

Half way through my daughter's kindergarten year, we relocated from our small town in Georgia to a larger town in Colorado. One reason God moved us, we now believe, was to put us in a new place to obtain the professional help we needed for our daughter. The new pediatrician we enlisted for general care observed our daughter and rightly concluded she showed evidence of hyperactivity, impulsivity, volatility, and distractibility well beyond expected norms for her age. Her emerging obsessions caused this humble doctor to refer our daughter immediately to a child psychiatrist. To his credit, he did not attempt to treat her himself.

Although we had identified a problem by age three, we were not knowledgeable enough to seek out the right professionals until she was age six. This pediatrician had wisely pointed us to our next step. This is the point in our story where we actually began to receive the specific help we needed.

Another lesson learned: General medical school education consists of a whopping six weeks of psychiatric instruction. Six weeks is inadequate training for treating the most complex organ in the human body, the brain. Nor is it adequate for prescribing psychiatric medications. So I urge you *not* to accept a pediatrician's or general (family) practitioner's prescription of brain chemistry medications, either for you or for your children, unless that doctor has sought out extensive additional specialized training. Instead, find a psychiatrist, the medical specialist who adequately understands brain chemistry, mental health, and drug interactions. For your child, select a psychiatrist who specializes in diagnosing and treating brain disorders in children. Specialized developmental pediatricians are another good option, especially in conjunction with a child psychiatrist.

Choosing the right professional initially could have spared my daughter from the effects of the incorrect medication, prescribed in ignorance by a general pediatrician. Brain chemistry medications require the knowledge of an up-to-date psychiatrist, not a general pediatrician. Some antidepressants, when incorrectly prescribed, can actually activate genetic predisposition to more serious psychiatric conditions. For example, with improper treatment, a person suffering with typical depression can escalate to a lifetime of bipolar depression.

> **Brain chemistry medications require the knowledge of an up-to-date psychiatrist, not a general pediatrician.**

In my daughter's case, the pediatrician did not recognize that Adderall, a stimulant often prescribed to children struggling with ADHD, was activating my daughter, the opposite desired effect. Adderall activated her because ADHD was secondary to Tourette's syndrome, a neurological condition exacerbated by stimulants. Mother's intuition and boldness spared my daughter further mishandling.

Through all of these trying times and our efforts to find the right professionals, my relationship with my husband remained exceptionally healthy in spite of the challenges we braved. Sadly, many parents who endure behavioral difficulties in their children also face additional challenges at home, among them tension between parents, separation, divorce, single parenting, and other forces that may create dysfunctionality in the home. These parents are more apt to blame the family environment or themselves for their children's struggles than to recognize a true underlying neurological condition and seek the help needed.

Mental Health Causes and Interventions to Consider

A Web site titled Church4EveryChild, created to help "churches pursue kids with mental illness, trauma or developmental disabilities and their families"[5] shares what one child psychiatrist offers as his theory to explain why one in every five children could be diagnosed with a mental health disorder based on symptom criteria. The article is called, "What's Causing the Epidemic of Mental Illness in Kids?" The author asserts that the rate of mental illness among children is

- A reflection of the struggle kids and families face in responding to the external demands placed upon them by our culture.
- A result of the general breakdown of the family…the maladaptive choices parents make in seeking to fill the emptiness in their lives with the concomitant consequences for kids.
- The consequence of a post-modern culture with an emphasis upon relative values and the lack of moral absolutes.
- The result of better recognition of symptoms of mental illness among educators and professionals.
- Caused by the interplay of environment and genetics.[6]

Cause impacts appropriate choice of treatment modalities, so each of these items is worthy of careful consideration. The response, however, is not always or initially to accept medication as the answer. It has been said that most American doctors have two solutions for health issues: pills or surgery. There is some truth to that criticism. Much has been written on the drugging of America. Big Pharma, a moniker for large drug firms, have built themselves a terrible reputation by using dangerous sales tactics that target practitioners treating children, seemingly profit driven.

Rather than a primary response being medicinal, behavioral interventions or family-based therapy can be appropriate treatments. Lack of available alternative treatment is often the cause of medications becoming the only intervention pursued when behavioral interventions may be appropriate, either in addition or instead of medication. With that said, family-based therapy or behavioral interventions alone cannot completely resolve a strictly biologically based mental health condition or other neurological hidden disability. Behavioral problems that are not caused by environment may not be rectifiable solely by counsel.

Over the past twenty years, neuroscience research has made great strides, thanks to the completion of DNA mapping. No longer are innovative health care professionals limited to a purely symptoms-based paradigm for diagnosis. It is now more possible to classify some psychiatric disorders through medical molecular biology, following in the footstep advances of neurology.

This less biased, thoroughly scientific approach removes the stigma of "character" or "parenting" blame-based mental health models that may still be assumed by some health care practitioners and the general public when mental health disorders are classified by symptoms only. Additionally and perhaps even more importantly, the emerging research of genetics and neurology is having profound impact on treatment choices.

Perceptions of the Uninformed

Unfortunately, uninformed observers may judge child behaviors as being strictly of volition, controllable by the child with effort and the responsibility of the parent to force the child into compliance. Labels such as ADHD, OCD, and even bipolar spectrum disorder (BSD) are considered by many people to be psychobabble, catchall phrases to make a medical syndrome out of poor parenting.

> Uninformed observers may judge child behaviors as being strictly of volition, controllable by the child with effort and the responsibility of the parent to force the child into compliance.

Adults who suffer with such disorders are often judged by the uninformed as defective in character, weak, or substandard individuals, untrustworthy and to be feared. Common media portrayals of those with such disabilities do not help the problem.

One bright exception to this overly generalized and negative portrayal was the 2002–2009 television series *Monk*,[7] which is about a brilliant San Francisco detective who both benefitted and suffered from OCD. Adrian Monk's idiosyncrasies were portrayed as both painful and endearing, creating respect plus empathy in the viewer's mind. The series addressed the problem of medicinal treatment for his condition as well. Medications dulled the detective's mind. He had to choose between his brilliance and his social acceptability, a common problem when trying to balance medications with side effects.

Historically conditions such as autism spectrum and Tourette's syndrome were speculated to be caused by parenting or character deficiencies. The famed psychoanalyst Sigmund Freud proposed such theories for brain disorders that were respected for forty to fifty years. These theories served as the prevailing thought, placing culpability on parenting or childhood experiences. He specifically blamed mothers for the emotional cause of autistic symptoms in their children.

In 1943, a highly respected psychiatrist from Johns Hopkins University, Leo Kanner, complemented Freud's assessment by coining the phrase "refrigerator mothers,"[8] a label cast disparagingly against the mothers of children with autism. Additionally during that era, Tourette's syndrome was blamed on psychosexual internal conflict, believed to be resultant from suppressed desire to masturbate. Although Sigmund Freud died in 1939, it was not until the 1970s that neurological or genetic causes were deemed a plausible explanation for disorders of the brain.

Medical society has been slow to change what were essentially unrighteous judgments against parents, especially mothers, and their children. The general public has been even slower. Perhaps slowest of all has been the church, an institution that still seems to insist that behavioral disorders of children can be resolved through parenting and submission to the discipline of a godly lifestyle. True, poor parenting and dysfunctional families can cause emotional disturbances in children. But organic, neurological, brain-based, behavioral disorders are not caused by parenting. And medical interventions by qualified specialists may be necessary.

Reflective Prayer

Heavenly Father,

With the professionals available to us in our town, with our insurance and financial situation, I ask for wisdom on how to proceed. "True wisdom and power are found" in You; "counsel and understanding" are Yours (Job 12:13). You say that I will "understand what is right," and I will "find the right way to go." I declare that Your wisdom is entering my heart, and Your knowledge is filling me with joy. Wise choices are watching over me. I decree that Your understanding is keeping my family safe (Proverbs 2:9–11). In Jesus' name I pray these words. Amen.

Chapter Seven

Medical Interventions

Any chapter on medical intervention will automatically date itself, hopefully, as advancements are made. Thanks to genome mapping, the understanding of brain biology is in a rapid advancements phase leading to new medical developments. Scientists are discovering how the code of DNA is expressed in the physical body, including in the brain.

As I felt in the beginning of my child raising challenges, many parents feel overwhelmed and ill equipped by the prospect of having to learn about medical or scientific research pertaining to special needs. Others understandably have little time to pursue research. I provide Web links in this chapter to aid parents in their search for answers.

Although this chapter by far is not a comprehensive discourse on available medical interventions and treatments for the vast variety of hidden disabilities, my goal is to provide a starting point to help impart vision for a path forward. Many different types of hidden disabilities exist, some of which may not be mentioned specifically by name in my writings. There are, however, multiple commonalities between the struggles faced by all parents raising children with such challenges. Providing information on some interventions may not be useful to every reader. But hopefully what is offered here will aid you in your pursuit for the interventions that work for you.

Philosophical Rumblings

Until fairly recently, psychiatry was based almost entirely on the study and characterization of symptoms alone. In this country, documentation for use by practicing psychiatrists existed as *The Diagnostic and Statistical Manual of the*

American Psychiatric Association (DSM), a medical resource informally called "the Bible of mental health." In the DSM, symptoms were clustered and named as psychiatric ailments.

Advancements in the fields of genetics and neurobiology have challenged this approach, creating a firestorm among practitioners, especially after the release of the latest edition. The DSM V is still based solely on symptoms. British psychologists have stirred the pot even more for a different

> Until fairly recently, psychiatry was based almost entirely on the study and characterization of symptoms alone.

reason than this objection expressed by some psychiatrists. Some British psychologists contest the biomedical model of mental illness. They contend that mental illness is not a physical pathology; rather, it is a function of environment and behavioral choices. As a result of the firestorm, in some settings psychology has become a rival professional field for treatment rather than a complementary one.

These philosophical rumblings are important for us to know because the fight still exists, even in the medical community, about the etiology and origin of hidden disabilities. Our struggle with stigma in the general public becomes all that much more difficult when mainstream publications quote naysayers who over-emphasize social or emotional causes of mental health disturbances, ignoring or downplaying the latest biological discoveries.

In the 1940s, the mother raising a child with autism was blamed for the child's disability but could not argue, as the prevalent thought of the day came from Freudian psychologists and not from neurobiologists. Now a fresh wave of the same kind of thinking popular half a century ago is challenging the neurology based, newest paradigm for mental health disorders. Pure social or emotional based models for mental health disturbances wrongly imply that psychology and psychiatry are diametrically opposed. The opposite is true. Both disciplines are needed and are complementary, not antagonistic.

Recent studies, for example, are showing actual physical changes in brain architecture of adults as the result of childhood abuse. The mechanism through which these brain changes occur, however, is still a mystery.[9] A research project by Emory University suggests chemical changes occur in DNA through trauma, meaning ancestral memory may then be passed to subsequent generations, potentially causing anxiety and phobia mental health disturbances.[10] These newest discoveries support the idea that psychiatrists and psychologists need to be in the same think tanks, brainstorming paths forward for those suffering with mental health challenges.

Hindrances to Getting the Right Help

As parents, what matters most to us in this new area of thought and discovery are the interventions that evolve from it. Equally important is how categorization of our children's conditions through any paradigm impacts treatment options and their costs.

Obtaining an official diagnosis aids parents in getting the right help for their children. Although it is not a federal requirement, children often are not eligible for special services in American schools without formal, documented diagnoses.

> **Although it is not a federal requirement, children often are not eligible for special services in American schools without formal, documented diagnoses.**

In addition to schools requiring diagnoses documentation to enable their interventions, insurance companies require diagnoses codes to qualify policyholders for treatment reimbursement. Sometimes, seemingly arbitrarily and variable from company to company, certain codes pay better than others. For example, OCD is a secondary diagnosis for most patients with Tourette's syndrome. Yet benefits are significantly better with some insurance companies when OCD is listed as the primary diagnosis, a determination that profoundly impacts reimbursement.

I discovered the pay component related to listing of the primary diagnosis quite by accident. Battle weary and struggling with discouragement, I decided to spend a few days at a Franciscan retreat center to pray, fast, and recharge spiritually. One insurance crisis required a call, so I kept that chore on my otherwise emptied schedule. When I made the call, I was in a tender place emotionally. Very uncharacteristic for me, I began crying on the phone as I poured out my heart to the woman answering my insurance questions. In response, she told me the dirty secret that I'm sure she was not allowed to disclose. My insurance provider had denied payment of my bills because Tourette's syndrome was listed as the primary diagnosis, not OCD. Apparently Tourette's did not pay, but OCD did.

For most of us, these subtleties of the insurance trade are either unknown to us or out of our control as we trudge our way through the system, fighting to bring relief to our children. Typically parents of children needing treatment must coordinate and seek treatment options on their own, using either self-pay or the known options within their insurance framework. With little to no bio-medical education or training in psychology, they research treatment modalities and insurance plans, determined to win the battle with school systems and insurance companies over the almighty dollar. They feel, and rightly so, that they are particularly vulnerable to the dictates of a system that rarely seems to have their children's best interests at heart. The financial toll adds to the stress.

As parents wade deep in the details, well-meaning friends join in the disorienting chorus, offering opinions on "evil pharmaceutical companies" and touting the propaganda claims of multi-level marketed "supplements" as viable mental treatments. I personally have experienced pitches from loved ones eager to help to purchase Blue Green Algae, Melaleuca, Acai Plus, Herbalife, Healthy Coffee USA, Juice Plus, Mannatech, Metabolife, Mona Vie, Protandim, and Essential Oils, just to name a few. These and other products like them are marketed with glowing testimonials and sometimes pseudo-science research that lacks the rigorous constraints of accepted methods for scientific scrutiny and validation.

With that said, I'd be lying if I pretended I hadn't tried any of these products for the sake of my children. An individual product may hold promise for those who can afford months long product trials. Desperation drives even those of us with science backgrounds to look beyond conventional options if the cost is low enough and risks are minimal. To date, none of the multi-level marketed products tried have achieved any measurable, positive results in my family. Although it is entirely plausible a product could prove beneficial, I am now choosing to wait for a broader consensus to claim efficacy than just listening to the accolades of those who gain financially from product sales.

Evidence-Based Treatments

A wiser path forward than trying interventions not supported by mental health practitioners is to choose evidence-based treatments. Evidence-based treatments are those that have been thoroughly vetted by the scientific community through reproducible demonstration that the treatments actually result in improvement. The Virginia Commission on Youth offers on its Web site a listing of evidence-based practices for young people with a need for mental health treatment.[11] This Web site and other similar governmental Web sites are a good place to start your reading. A quality child psychiatrist also can provide a wealth of knowledge to help you choose which interventions affordable to you are most likely to be effective.

My navigation through those early years of medical intervention was fraught with vexation. My husband and I decided, in conjunction with my daughter's physicians, that some form of medication was warranted. I remember those days when I had to bridle my response to overt and crass judgment by observers on my most sacred call: to parent my children to the best of my knowledge and ability. The incredulous asking of the question, "You want to drug your child?" masked an underlying belief of the questioner: my child raising skills were nonexistent; I was too lazy to exert the effort necessary to train my children; or my shallowness and poor character had enticed me to drug my children as a substitute for parenting.

I haven't met an individual who condemns the use of medication for treating Parkinson's disease or Alzheimer's. Those conditions are brain based, and everyone seems to know it. What people don't seem to know is that many hidden disabilities are also brain based, organic in nature.

You may hear that coconut oil, for example, can help Parkinson's or Alzheimer's; but using doctor prescribed medications for these disorders incurs no wrath from friends, families, or church members. What happens, however, when you announce that your child is starting a medication trial for volatility, debilitating depression, oppositional defiance, obsessions, or inability to focus? Critics rise up to offer their opinions. "Your children are pawns of the corporate greed of pharmaceutical companies," they exclaim with faux authoritative oomph. Or with more carefully chosen words than the outright "Have you tried discipline?" or "Have you tried prayer?" they express those same ideas, contesting your decision to medicate.

Treating disorders of the brain may require a holistic approach for success, just as treating cardiac disorders does. A cardiologist may discuss evidence-based interventions such as behavioral (exercise) and dietary changes to augment the recommended medicinal treatment. He also may suggest certain supplements. Few people eye this multi-faceted management approach with suspicion for cardiac patients, yet when children present with a disadvantageous neurological difference, many people feel compelled to say medicinal treatments are evil and a substitute for parenting. These opposite judgments point to a serious breakdown of logic at the very least. Judging mental illness with an unwarranted harshness only adds to the pain and confusion a family dealing with mental health challenges endures.

Pushing into Future Advancements

Brain chemistry is complex science. Many psychiatrists do not keep up to date with the latest research even though brain science is their specialty. It is wise, therefore, to find a psychiatrist with strong credentials and recommendations to diagnose your child. If you discover your choice psychiatrist relying solely on interviews and discussions of symptoms without the latest research information, you may be in for antiquated or hit-or-miss drug trials. Choose instead a psychiatrist conversant with the latest discoveries, especially as they relate to sleep medicine, genetic testing, and brain SPECT imaging.

> Brain chemistry is complex science. Many psychiatrists do not keep up to date with the latest research even though brain science is their specialty.

Sleep study evaluations can rule out primary sleep disorders that cause secondary symptoms of psychiatric disturbance. Although this discovery dates back over at least a decade, many mental health practitioners still do not explore this consideration. Even though the connection between sleep disorders and psychiatric symptoms is not considered particularly controversial, some psychiatrists still choose not to include sleep study evaluation as part of their assessment and diagnosis.

Hyperactivity, impulsivity, inattentiveness, and even depression symptoms can all result from the disruption of the body's natural restorative sleep processes. When diagnoses are based on symptoms alone rather than through using sleep studies, genetic testing, and looking at the actual brain, children with primary sleep disorders may be misdiagnosed with conditions such as ADHD. Sleep disorders are more prevalent in higher altitudes, so a move to a different region may even be the underlying catalyst for a child's change in behavior.

It appalls me that many psychiatrists still ignore sleep medicine when evidence-based articles were posted in scientific journals of medicine on the subject as far back as the 1980s, if not longer. It may be twenty years before the bulk of psychiatrists incorporate the newest developments into their practices. Of course by then, they will no longer *be* the newest developments.

An even newer advancement in the diagnosis and treatment of mental health disorders than sleep medicine is genetic testing. Genetic testing has the power to dramatically impact psychiatric care. It takes the theoretical prospect of DNA characterization that the general population has heard about in broad terms and actually supplies this cutting edge technology to physicians and mental health practitioners.

To my knowledge, currently only one company is offering genetic testing for use in psychiatric treatment to the medical commercial market. Genomind is the company bringing new innovations in genetic testing to help doctors treat brain chemistry problems more effectively. The Genocept™ Assay is a "simple to use saliva-based tool for clinicians to understand the genetic markers that best inform patient responses to different psychiatric treatments."[12] It is taking much of the guesswork out of drug trials to treat brain chemistry disorders. As of the spring of 2014, the assay identifies ten biomarkers. Within a year, the test offered should be available to identify over thirty different alleles, alternative forms of a gene responsible for inheritance variation, which impact mental health diagnosis and treatment.

Trying Something New

My family began with fully vetted, evidence-based treatments; however, I was not willing to wait twenty years for every assessment available to become conventional or orthodox prior to consideration. We chose as well to explore Brain SPECT scans (Single Photon Emission Computed Tomography) as an aid to determining which medications or supplements my son should take to help him with his tics, OCD, and ADHD. I had come to see that branching out to try non-evidence-based treatments is a viable path forward after more accepted treatments have been exhausted and fail to yield satisfactory progress. Sometimes evidence is accumulating in favor of an intervention, but still not in sufficient quantity for the rigorous scientific scrutiny needed to be considered an evidence-based treatment.

Impressed by supporting documentation, my son and I flew all the way from Colorado to Atlanta to see if the additional information gleaned from a SPECT scan available there could impact his treatment positively. After a neurologist read my son's scan of brain activity, he recommended widely available supplements as well as medications through matching efficacy with the specific scan pattern (rather than solely on symptoms).

The clinic's prescriptive recommendations, to date, have been the most helpful input my son has received relating to treatment. My son, as a result, has been off all prescription medications for a year, with fewer symptoms troubling him than ever before.

Brain SPECT imaging is technology that looks at cerebral blood flow related to brain functioning. Daniel Amen, MD, has done extensive correlations of scans with symptoms supporting the theory of biological basis for behaviors.[13] Although many naysayers question the validity of using brain SPECT imaging in diagnosis and treatment of psychiatric disorders, the stats are in Dr. Amen's favor for bringing a higher quality of life to those who have not been helped through more mainstream psychiatry. Dr. Amen's commonly reprinted claim, "Psychiatry remains the only medical specialty that rarely looks at the organ it treats"[14] makes a good point. Brain SPECT imaging may be a treatment impacting diagnostic tool that would interest you as well.

The prescriptive recommendations from the clinic my son and I visited emphasized the use of specifically targeted supplements first, to be followed by targeted medications if the supplementation did not provide adequate relief from symptoms. I learned that just because a supplement is generally labeled "for brain health" does not mean it is useful for a child's specific condition. It may wrongly activate an area of the brain that is already overactive or calm a portion of the brain that is already underactive. I did not realize prior to this testing that supplementation therapy, without brain activity scan information, was as hit-or-miss a prospect as the drug trials recommended by some psychiatrists.

One of my son's local specialists brought up an important consideration about supplements. Because of lack of adequate regulation, not all supplements actually contain what they purport. When choosing supplementation, it is best to pay the higher price for National Science Foundation certification that ensures product and ingredient safety. The National Institutes of Health, Office of Dietary Supplements, has an informative Web site that can strengthen your knowledge and understanding of dietary supplementation.[15]

Brain SPECT scans showing functional activity of the brain can answer a lot of questions and guide us in our reactions to our children's behaviors. My son's brain SPECT showed two holes of inactivity the size of quarters in his prefrontal cortex, the part of his brain needed to concentrate. At rest that part of his brain was active, but when he tried to focus, it shut off. It was like Curly's declaration in The Three Stooges, "I'm tryin' to think, but nothin' happens!" The more pressure I exerted to get my son to "focus harder" on schoolwork, the more his mis-wired brain shut off.

I have seen functional imaging brain scans of children with severe ADHD during attempted concentration that look like most of the prefrontal cortex was missing. I'm grateful for the scientific breakthroughs that have made these scans available. These scans provide critical information for parents to have when determining how to respond to their children's average to high intelligence yet poor academic performance.

Why Not Seek Help?

Who are the untouchables in our society? Who are the outcasts for whom even the church seems to lack grace or faith? Why are people afraid of individuals with behavior outside the norm of typical?

Possibly the stigma and fear we and our children face from others is because scientific breakthroughs on brain chemistry research are not yet widely known by the general public. The behavioral choice based models (it's the fault of the parents, and so on) still seem to control the judgments of the uninformed. As parents of children with hidden disabilities, we can be part of the solution, advocating for all who endure not only the challenges of brain differences but also the unrighteous judgments of others.

What are the effects of these judgments against the innocent children who suffer already with hidden disabilities? The fear and judgments of the uninformed isolate those who suffer. They also keep parents from admitting there may be an issue when a child has continual and unresolvable behavior problems. As a result, fear and judgment sway the parents' decision to refuse medical intervention or even to seek a professional opinion.

A child needing behavioral intervention or medical intervention, including pharmaceuticals, is not ideal. But that assessment as a negative judgment is part of the problem with elevating the ideal. It blocks parents from accepting life as it is and making the best decisions based on the reality of their circumstances.

What I hear most in parents of children with hidden disabilities is not always pure inability to accept the real instead of the ideal or unwillingness to sacrifice and make intervention happen. Instead it is cynicism. Parents become cynical regarding the pharmaceutical industry, develop an aversion to medications, or come to distrust all doctors as a result of the failure of some. Churches wrongly counsel families to look only inward (behavioral choices) and upward (to God) for resolution, discouraging parents from seeking professional help. I also hear parents judging and blaming themselves because of a divorce, less than stellar family dynamics, or parenting inconsistencies. They wrongly believe if *they* just try harder, their children will straighten out.

When you do not seek help when something clearly is physiologically wrong with your child—a brain based neurological difference that you deny by refusal to seek elucidation or intervention, all the while still holding that child to the same standards as peers or siblings—you send the wrong message to that child. Whether spoken aloud or not, that message is, "You are to blame for these behaviors. Your lack of success in resolving your issues is your own fault." As a result of your choices, your child is left alone to manage the problem, bound for failure and the self-loathing that accompanies it.

How much better is it for you and your child to get clarity about what is wrong, take ownership of the matter, and seek interventions, possibly including supplements and medications, as needed? How much more life-giving and reality based are these choices than allowing fear, judgment, cynicism, or protection of the idol of the ideal to dictate your response to your struggling child?

Don't allow yourself to be lulled into inaction because of the fluctuation of brain chemistry in your child, those good days when you try to convince yourself that your child truly is typical and there isn't a medical problem after all. Understandably, somehow that choice can seem better than admitting your child may have the unthinkable, what you might feel is the leprosy equivalent in today's hierarchy of unacceptable conditions. Instead, consider the cost to your child, let go of your fears and judgments, and seek life-giving intervention.

Reflective Prayer

Heavenly Father,

Forgive me for my delay in seeking intervention, for when my reluctance was not born out of what was best for my child. At times I have felt immobilized. And so I offer to You my fears and judgments against neurological issues I do not fully understand. I commit to rely upon Your grace (Acts 13:43). With Your grace, I receive Your peace (1 Corinthians 1:3).

Release Your friendship and counsel over my child's bedroom, that Your lamp would shine above and upon his/her head, that he/she would walk through the darkness by Your light (Job 29:3–4). In Jesus' name I pray these words. Amen.

Chapter Eight

The Fight for Education

Almost immediately after entering kindergarten, my daughter with hidden disabilities began having difficulties in her private school. We had moved across country halfway through her kindergarten year, so I decided to homeschool her and her third grade sister to lessen the sorrow of relocation for my girls. A few months after the move, my son was born, adding to my joy but also adding to the stress of co-joining parenting with homeschooling. I persevered for two years, until I could go on no longer. That's when the fight for education for my daughter with special needs began.

During those two years of homeschooling, I discovered several questions I needed to have asked myself and answered about homeschooling a child with disabilities. Was I basing my decision to homeschool solely on what was best for my child with special needs? At what cost to the rest of the family was I homeschooling this one, and was that cost a fair trade for the other family members? And lastly, did I have the expertise to offer my child the extra interventions needed; and if not, did I have the time and fortitude to learn quickly?

At first I did not know to ask myself those questions. I believed strongly that homeschooling was the best option for my younger daughter. At the time of my decision to stop homeschooling her, I was just beginning to work with a child psychiatrist to understand her behavior and to identify the disability. I had pushed through the challenges gallantly, ignoring my own needs, until I found myself curled up in a fetal position in a pile of dirty laundry, sobbing uncontrollably. One afternoon's emotional breakdown was all I needed to recognize that a change in my stress level and my daughter's education provider was mandatory.

From Failure to the Right Choice

I had convinced myself that my middle child needed to be homeschooled; therefore, initially I saw no other options for her. She struggled with extreme volatility, excessive obsessive behaviors, sensory issues, and incontinence as well as lacking the emotional maturity of her equals in age by several years. On the positive side of the scale, by the time she was in the second grade, she was already decoding words on an eleventh grade level (I had her tested). The contrast between her advanced intellectual functioning and delayed physical and social abilities was stark, creating tension between her and her peers. So how could I send her back into a classroom full of children and expect her to do well?

> I had convinced myself that my middle child needed to be home-schooled; therefore, initially I saw no other options for her.

At age eight, my daughter was horribly vulnerable, completely oblivious to the impact her behaviors had on others. Her open-hearted, loving nature meant she was particularly sensitive to rejection. She internalized the messages from scowling faces, considering them not as a normal response to her rages but as a sign of her own lack of worth or like-ability. Even as I enrolled her, I worried about how my daughter would fare integrated with other students for eight hours a day, five days a week.

I hated myself for what I thought was "failing" as a parent to my daughter. What did failure look like for this Type A mother? Anything that fell short of "the ideal." The ideal was homeschooling. I had already homeschooled her for half of kindergarten, all of first grade, and half of second. I also had homeschooled my oldest daughter. Meanwhile, I'd had a baby, lived in a new town with next to no friends, and struggled to attend most church functions or social events to create friends.

Yet I also knew mainstreaming her in the neighborhood school was my only viable path forward. Because public schools, including charter schools, receive federal money, they have a statutory obligation to comply with laws governing education for those with disabilities. In other words, in the public schools, my daughter would have to receive the accommodations she needed.

By the time I came to my homeschool meltdown, I had a fifth grader, a toddler, and a screaming and volatile second grader. Although I had a very supportive husband, I did not have adequate emotional or internal spiritual resources to continue homeschooling my daughter with hidden disabilities. So I made the right but difficult choice. I put my daughter in public school.

To be honest, I really didn't do it for her. I did it for my mental health. I did it for my other daughter, whom I continued to homeschool and build relationship with for the next five years. I did it for my son. I did it for my husband.

It was the hardest thing I had ever done because at the time I thought it wasn't what was "ideal" for my middle daughter. I loved her just as desperately as I loved all the other members of my family. But my decision was right, and the idol of ideal came crashing down.

Assessments

I had already invested time and money to identify my daughter's disabilities and abilities. I had paperwork from her extensive Independent Educational Evaluation (IEE) completed and in hand at enrollment. I knew nothing about special education law, my daughter's rights, or what to expect from her new school. In spite of my ignorance, somehow I had done something else right. I had not chosen to rely on the public school system for testing and evaluation that would form the foundation of behavioral or academic interventions for my daughter. Instead, I had sought and obtained professional assessments and evaluations elsewhere.

I knew, no matter how stellar the school district, no teacher or administrator would love or care about my daughter as deeply as I did. Their evaluative choices were more likely to reflect the district's needs over the needs of my daughter. The testing I had obtained independently was exactly what my daughter needed. In the years that followed, anytime the school district paid for a service for the benefit of my daughter or my son, I considered the covered expense a bonus. I expected to pay for evaluations or services myself and inform the school of our efforts.

One example is when my son's language scores began to drop in the fourth grade as longer prose was expected to flow from his pencil. Trouble with the act of writing was creating frustration for my son, even though he was excellent in spelling, sentence structure, and expression of ideas. He just couldn't make his pencil move to express what was in his brilliant mind. The school offered no intervention, but I knew intervention was needed.

I obtained an assessment from an assistive technology expert to determine appropriate interventions. I took that assessment report to his school, hoping the school would supply the necessary hardware. Although it was available on a district level, the school was disinterested in jumping through the necessary hoops to obtain the equipment loans. So I purchased my son a laptop and used the assistive technology documentation to successfully argue for the integration of the laptop into my son's accommodations, along with changes in routine when my son took standardized national tests. As a parent, I identified the problem and through great financial difficulty, paid for resolution myself.

You as the parent have the right to request assessment through your child's public school for a possible disability relating to academic struggles experienced by your child. When a parent makes a request for an evaluation, it is mandatory by law for the school to provide the assessment. If the school refuses, you must be given written notice explaining the denial. In spite of legal requirements, schools do not always do so.

> You as the parent have the right to request assessment through your child's public school for a possible disability relating to academic struggles experienced by your child.

It is possible the school may actually initiate testing based on observed issues with your child (testing to be commenced only upon your informed consent). One advantage of a school-administered assessment is cost. Parents do not pay for the testing. Another advantage is "buy in," because schools may be more impressed by their own testing results than results obtained through external providers.

Success to get schools to order the assessments a parent deems critical varies state by state. In Colorado, when I believed my son needed a speech evaluation in the second grade, the school informed me that only the bottom three percent of children with speech problems qualified for intervention. My son wasn't "bad enough" to qualify, so the school did not evaluate my son's speech problem. In response, I independently took my son to a speech pathologist, who evaluated him for his consistent mispronunciation of r-controlled vowels. The school remained uninvolved.

Although these two examples show how my son's school did not offer the assessment or intervention I desired for him, overall the public school system was very cooperative and interested in the success of my children. For example, several teachers surrendered their own personal time after school on a regular basis to help my son reach goals, and teachers studied material I provided about my children's disabilities. I had an excellent working relationship with both teachers and administrators. I intervened for my children in ways that gave me the opportunity to express continuously my empathy for those who educated my children and the hurdles they faced with funding and time constraints.

Required by Law

Schools are required by national law, through the Individuals with Disabilities Education Improvement Act (IDEA), to provide services for children with disabilities when they need special education and related services because of one or more conditions. An excellent resource available to use for reference to aid you in understanding your rights as a parent of a child with a disability is a book titled, *Wrightslaw: Special Education Law.*[16] The problem with the law is that not every child with a hidden disability qualifies for special education.

Every student who qualifies to receive special education services must have a directive plan, the Individualized Education Program (IEP), which describes educational goals and available support to reach those goals. If your child qualifies, as a parent you have the right to be part of the team that sets your child's objectives for the academic year.

Protections for students are greater under IDEA than they are under another provision, Section 504; however, IEPs do not follow the child into college. A 504 behavior plan does. Most if not all children who qualify for an IEP also qualify for a Section 504 plan, so a child can move from an IEP to a Section 504 plan for college.

The 504 behavior plan concept was born out of the anti-discrimination statute called Section 504, a part of the Rehabilitation Act of 1973. This federal statute is mandatory, but implementation may look different from state to state. The purpose of Section 504 is to ensure that those with disabilities receive equal access to education through provision of accommodations.

Fortunately for me, my children with hidden disabilities both had a 504 behavior plan for the entirety of their educational years. What it meant to me was homework modification, a safe place for my children to retreat when ticcing during school hours, and other classroom interventions specific to their needs. Even permission to wear a hat in class can be requested for sensory sensitivity as a 504 accommodation.

With an IEP or a 504 behavioral plan or both in place, your child may still struggle with trying to compensate for her or his disability. And those who oversee your child may not properly interpret the internal battles your child is navigating. As I did, you may find yourself disagreeing strongly with the conclusions of school appointed interventionists.

Drawing Battle Lines

When my son was in the first grade, his classmates were mostly accepting and his teacher understanding. Yet his vocal and motor tics still caused him embarrassment. Unwanted and humiliating vocal sounds happened repeatedly, every single day. He learned to cover for himself through comical behaviors.

When the school psychologist came to observe my son in the classroom, the clowning behaviors were noted. The psychologist's assessment, as a result, included the judgment that my son was an attention seeker. Really? Exactly the opposite was the truth. His jester behaviors in the midst of vocal or motor tics were to conceal the tics.

The more controlled my son's gross and fine motor movements became for him as he aged, the more obvious the unwanted movements or sounds became. His clowning antics were actually attempts to disappear, not to draw attention to himself.

Sometimes the specific tics were downright humiliating. For a painfully prolonged several weeks, my son had a complex motor tic of slamming his fist into his groin in a knockout punch. He neither enjoyed this nor thought it was funny. He was mortified, humiliated, and in pain. So he could have died a thousand deaths when the school psychologist assassinated his intentions by labeling him simply as attention seeking.

Mischaracterizations such as this one tempted me as a parent to go "Mama Bear" on my children's overseers. A level head with aim for advocacy was wiser. I pretended that school officials and I were all on the same team and believed in my son or in my daughter as much as I did. Visualization was a powerful tool that helped me keep my cool!

Needed loyalties were created when I offered grace in communicating how classroom observers were getting it wrong. I employed face-saving maneuvers. There were times this grace took as much self-discipline as I used when my obstetrician told me, "Don't push!" When battle lines had to be drawn for a serious fight, the more warriors I retained on my side of the chalk line through amassed loyalties, the better. With intentionality, I put the issue on one side of the battle line and the school officials with myself on the other.

Schools must provide, under IDEA, a free and appropriate public education (FAPE) accommodating disabilities. But FAPE is not synonymous with providing the absolute best education available for children with special needs. Although parents may have complaints against their child's school or district, the school may or may not be liable under law to oblige the parents' demands. The best way to ensure appropriate accommodations, I learned, is to build a quality relationship with your child's educators.

Knowing When and How to Fight

I learned it is best to avoid adversarial confrontations, no matter how correct you believe your position. In my mind, disrespect toward school representatives is never acceptable behavior for a Christian honoring God's value system, even in defense of a child. An excellent resource to aid you in a respectable fight is *Wrightslaw: Emotions to Advocacy: The Special Education Survival Guide*.[17] This book is a classic for parents of children with disabilities who are navigating through rights and expectations in regard to the school system. Take the time to learn your rights under the law. Additional helpful information may be found on the Wrightslaw Web site[18].

The time may come, if you are in a particularly unresponsive or ignorant school district, that a legal battle becomes enticing in order to assure access to appropriate educational opportunities or accommodations for your child. Even when parents fully understand their rights under the law, however, access to justice may still be elusive. An excellent Web resource created by a special education attorney from Telios Law exists for parents in Colorado who are addressing options.[19] Although some laws differ from state to state, the general guidelines on this site offered for access to justice are extremely informative, since statutes relating to education and disabilities are federally mandated.

Legal battles have their costs. A better option may be a special education parent advocate that can help you negotiate with the school. Advocates can be recommended through local organizations that serve people with disabilities or through private counselors. Advocates are not required to possess any form of certification, so their counsel comes mostly from experience. If they do not have a good grasp of the complexities of the law, however, they may be ineffectual.

A disability lawyer can also advocate with the school in addition to giving legal advice that clarifies potential next steps. A next step can be to take action by filing a complaint with the Office of Civil Rights or perhaps request mediation from your state's Department of Education.

If you are still unsatisfied with resolution of a grievance, you can file a state-level complaint or file a due process complaint notice. Due process complaint notices cost several thousand dollars to file, but if you are in the right, the school usually capitulates at that point and provides at least some level of service. For a complex situation, the battle may be worth the expenditure. A due process complaint usually resolves once it is filed, with only about one in ten progressing to a due process hearing.

A due process hearing can cost upwards of sixty thousand dollars out of pocket expense. Sometimes attorneys will go forward pro bono (free) or count on shifting attorney fees if you win. Personally I think I'd rather take that cash and buy another house in a better school district!

Just once I was sorely tempted to file an Office of Civil Rights complaint against a charter school that sent me a letter clearly stating that my son's high school admission was denied due to a sleep apnea diagnosis. I sent a respectful letter informing the school that it had broken the law, but I took no further action. Because I chose not to engage the Dean of Admissions while I was upset, I did not say anything I would later regret. I chose what, in retrospect, was a better school placement for my son. And I was free to expend my energies instead on child raising efforts.

I managed to survive the school years without taking any legal actions. Knowing when and how to fight saved me from many potentially difficult and costly battles. It is up to you and your best judgments, given your unique circumstances, to determine your path forward.

Reflective Prayer

Heavenly Father,

I ask for Your mercy in all the ways I feel I have failed my child. I offer up to You my ideals of perfection that cause me such pain. As I fight for the rights of my child, I commit to honoring You in the midst of the battle.

I declare in Jesus' name that true justice prevails over access to accommodations as required for my child by law. You, O righteous Lord, love justice (Psalm 11:7). I decree that my family's innocence will "radiate like the dawn," and the justice of our "cause will shine like the noonday sun" (Psalm 37:6). I commit our struggles in the battle for education to You, trusting You and knowing You will help us (Psalm 37:5). In Jesus' name I pray these words. Amen.

Chapter Nine

Life without Regrets

Some days every ounce of my child raising feels like wasted effort. I see no reward, no payback, and no fruit from grueling discussions, patience, or persistence. On those days, my children behave irrationally, unreasonably, ridiculously—as though they have gone their whole lives without any values instilled or any input from me whatsoever. In spite of such times, I've discovered, there is a way to live without regrets.

I've generalized my understanding of human nature as well, after processing through those days that seem to lack evidence of my investment of love and training into the lives of my children. I've abandoned the idea that I can control how *any* human being behaves or processes, including my own children. The most I can hope for is to influence others for their own benefit, for the good of those around them, or for the advancement of the Kingdom of God.

As for me, my personal goal in relation to family dynamics is to live my own life well, to live life with no regrets. Living life without regrets can be done no matter what the circumstances, no matter how poorly you or I have been treated by others of *any* age. There is one thing I can control—myself.

> **Living life without regrets can be done no matter what the circumstances, no matter how poorly you or I have been treated.**

One morning I successfully controlled how I responded as I was attacked verbally because I had expressed my disapproval of legalized marijuana, citing brain scans of heavy users. In the middle of this family conversation, if it could be called that, my son walked dismissively out of the kitchen, ending what had started as a perfectly enjoyable breakfast meal together as a family. His older sister had just rampaged, defending her Internet friends who, although on welfare, "deserved" a recreational drug "just like everyone else." Apparently she believed legalization of marijuana was a benefit to them. Although not a user of any illegal substances, she felt passionately about the topic.

My son had seen the wild rage in his sister's eyes, knew it well, and so dismissed her entirely. His walking out of the room cast the equivalent of a pint of gasoline on an already engaged inferno of my daughter's self-immolation.

I followed my son out of the room, explaining to him that during his whole life he would encounter people who expressed their outrage and disagreements with vitriol and loud protests. Using skills that caused another person to feel heard, I told him, would minimize the intensity of those encounters. If he discerned he must excuse himself in order to maintain his self-control, he could do so respectfully "because of the honorable man you have chosen to be." And "setting boundaries is healthy behavior," I added, to determine internally what he would and would not tolerate. So also was deciding not to become a willing recipient of another's vile verbal effluence.

My preference, I said, was for him to address his sister in a calm voice that reflected her valid dignity as a person. I would have liked for him to have said, even if his sister had screamed over him, "I'm sorry. I am not willing to have this conversation. It is time for me to get ready for school. Excuse me." He then could have left the room courteously, without any culpability whatsoever.

Although I considered the breakfast exchange most unpleasant, it was a moment of no regrets for me. And this was exactly the type of moment that can inspire revelation for my children. Although like me, they cannot control other people, they *can* live their own lives without regrets, regardless of the behaviors of others at home, school or eventually in the workplace.

Ensuing Conversations behind Closed Doors

How we deal with life behind the closed doors of home packs our bag of resources for how we deal with life outside of the safety of our home. Having to deal with inappropriate communication is not ideal, but it is doable and has benefits. In my house, we are afforded many trial runs on how to deal honorably with stressful or abusive situations. My children and I can, and do, use such situations as excellent life training. They teach us to rise above the disrespectful, domineering moments of others each of us may encounter in the future, standing firm on principles of uprightness and self-control. Each of us can learn grace under pressure.

When my daughter's chemistry shifts back to peaceable after an outburst, we continue to work together on learning to accept with grace the differing perspectives and viewpoints of others. She then has the opportunity to explore respectful ways to communicate her need to feel heard and to avoid being dismissed as she expresses passionate ideas. The perspective in post-incident conversation does not have to be just on ways family members have failed, but on what each can learn from their own behaviors.

My discussion with my son after he walked away from the table was less about his sister's outburst and more about his success in drawing clear boundaries and his growth potential in learning to draw them in the future. It was about choosing respectful communication over silence. My conversation with my daughter that day was less about the perceived rudeness of her brother's dismissive exit and more about the validity of differing opinions, including hers. A pleasant tone, devoid of flailing, I said, could have avoided the dispersion of safety in conversation the family had all felt thirty seconds prior to her eruption.

My daughter's life is difficult. She can't bear the weight of her brother's learning curve, or even mine for that matter. My son cannot bear the weight of his sister's fight for mental stability. I cannot bear the weight of my own children's need to succeed in their battles with life's challenges. None of us need the drama. What each of us can do, however, is expend the bulk of our energies on how we choose to live our own lives, with dignity and respect for all, regardless of what assails us. It is a difficult proposition for us as parents, because we feel the brunt of responsibility to assure our children get life right.

> **What each of us can do, however, is expend the bulk of our energies on how we choose to live our own lives, with dignity and respect for all, regardless of what assails us.**

Our greatest responsibility as parents, I have learned, is to live our own lives, in the face of all our challenges, without regret. I do it by loving, teaching, training, and holding my children accountable, all the while using self-control. My children's ultimate outcome, however, is something over which I honestly have no direct control. But I can control myself.

For typical families, the desired outcome seems deceptively clear as a direct correlation. The parents love, teach, and train. The children become God fearing, loving, emotionally healthy, and competent adults. The occasional exception can be rightfully or wrongfully pinned to presumed parental failures or the "bad child" who had everything but threw it all away.

On those difficult days, when all seems for naught, I must know that my life has been lived well and with honor. Behind closed doors, where no one else except my family members see or hear, my responses to my screaming children must be above reproach. And when my responses are not, I must humbly apologize for my behaviors—not in contrast to the behaviors of others, but solely on the merits of my own choices.

Justification has no place in our parenting, in our marriages, or in the totality of how we regulate our lives. How we behave is not in response to how others behave. We behave based on who we are as children of the Most High God. We live our lives for an audience of One. In doing so, we can live our lives without regrets, holding our heads high.

Remain above Reproach

My first allegiance is to my God. This decision means that my role as a mother must be submitted to the loving scrutiny of my Creator, who desires the best for both me *and* for my children. It also means that my parenting isn't behind closed doors after all. It is a public matter as far as celestial beings are concerned. I consider my life to have a "cloud of witnesses" (Hebrews 12:1).

My decision probably sounds all well and good and straightforward enough for parents raising typical babies and small children that sit in their laps and listen to Bible story books. But for those raising a child with a mental illness, a developmental disability, or even a very mixed up typical teen, the decision is a whole other story.

A casual friend of mine called from California to share her latest crisis with her neurologically typical teenaged child, the youngest of four and her only girl. The daughter was in a therapeutic residential facility. My daughter had been in one twice before, which made me a good sounding board to my friend. But the conversation caused me to ponder the cost of indulging ourselves in less than helpful responses based on our frustrations.

As a parent, no matter how violent, unreasonable, or oppositional my child becomes, I have a responsibility to remain above reproach. Even parents of typical teens can find themselves speaking too harshly or making a comment they later regret. But oh, how much more tempting it can be to respond badly when disciplining a child with hidden disabilities after consistent parenting techniques appear to be of no avail!

In those moments of exasperation, I'm assailed by a temptation to throw all restraint to the wind. But I can't. After those times, when I realize I crossed over and said too much, I return to my child and ask forgiveness. I remind myself that I ascribe to the 90/10 principle, which means that I am still responsible for my ten percent, even if the other person was ninety percent guilty. It is humbling to apologize to a child who has just cleared tabletops, thrown furniture, or even put holes in the wall for the past two hours; but it is right. In that moment of expressed regret, it is no longer about what the child did. It is about what I did that was wrong.

> I remind myself that I ascribe to the 90/10 principle, which means that I am still responsible for my ten percent, even if the other person was ninety percent guilty.

How can we as parents hold our children accountable to a standard of self-control that we are not willing to submit to ourselves? My friend's phone call revealed that as her daughter became more difficult, she resorted to calling the child a "wretch." Then over time, this indiscretion became, "Bitch!" From that point on, what authority did she have left to demand any level of respect or verbal control from her offspring?

Mistakes Happen

When we abandon self-control, failing to bridle our own tongues or control our own behaviors without repentance, we tie our parenting hands. How can we then attempt to persuade our children that allowing God's Holy Spirit to rule our lives has any relevance to them? Our words become distasteful, ineffectual religion to our children.

It is not that mistakes don't happen. They do. It's about what to do when mistakes happen.

At age five, my daughter still wet herself consistently. The urologist had insisted she was perfectly healthy. The pediatrician had claimed she was just caught up in playing, which was more important to her than using a potty. I had tried everything recommended by every book I could find. I had practiced the suggestions consistently, in spite of inconvenience. We had the potty M&M'S; we had the positive reinforcement; we had the pee-pee charts. We had the entertaining storybooks outlining the procedure, and we began not too early but also not too late. Yet after all my efforts of consistent training, she was still wetting and occasionally even soiling herself.

I began resorting to more drastic measures beyond Love and Logic parenting techniques. I made her leave fun places when it happened. I threw away her favorite panties decorated with Baby Bop when she soiled them, citing a lack of ability to wash them. I warned her beforehand always that consequences would follow her actions, yet each time she was devastated by the consequences, as though they had come unprovoked. I, on the other hand, was becoming cold— and seeped in frustration.

One afternoon as I sat on my bedroom floor, my daughter approached me with wet panties. I took them off of her, not roughly, and then I put them close to her face, saying something very stern about her "choice" to keep wetting. I shocked myself. My actions were disrespectful and motivated out of frustration. I was out of line, even if every bit of her wetting had been intentional.

I began weeping over my indiscretion. I held her close and apologized profusely. I explained to her why what I had done was wrong. Parents must treat children with respect, just as children must treat others with respect. Thankfully my daughter's generous nature resulted in immediate forgiveness.

Later I would discover to my chagrin that her incontinence was secondary to Sensory Integration Disorder, a relatively common ailment that often accompanies developmental disabilities. The incident is not a painful memory for her. She laughs on the rare occasion that I bring it up and swears she doesn't recall it at all. But what if I hadn't had the humility to repent, in front of her, in real time?

What happens when we indulge ourselves by falling into a pattern of verbal, emotional, or even physical abuse of our children? We absolutely negate our parenting authority in the eyes of the children. Later, even when we respond well to our children while holding them accountable, they feel lessened responsibility to submit because of our previous infractions.

Lesson learned: When mistakes happen, and they will, be quick to repent. Your authority and spiritual credibility with your children depend on it.

Misrepresentation

There are times, however, when children distort a scenario to appear as though they are victims even after we have responded appropriately to a very difficult situation. When it happens, parents of children with special needs can feel as if they are at the brink of a Department of Human Services (DHS) call. They worry, and rightfully so, about their children's dramatized retellings to others, creating an even more compelling parental need to be above reproach no matter what.

When my daughter was in the fifth grade, she threw one of her rage attacks, putting my husband and I on the brink. Whenever these attacks happened, nothing was safe. She routinely cleared tabletops, threw furniture, kicked, screamed, and otherwise destroyed the peaceful atmosphere for the rest of the household. The uninformed might think these extreme scenarios would be brought on by a huge perceived offense against her, but they could result from something as minor as being stuck with the end slice of bread as her piece of toast.

On this particular occasion, my husband and I resolutely requested that she retire to her room. We were familiar with the scenario and had learned she would break fewer items when left alone, without an audience and surrounded by her own personal belongings. She refused and chose plan B, whereby we would physically remove her from the public living area and put her in her room. It had happened many times before.

Her father, calmly for the situation and as gently as possible, pinned her wailing, writhing body and flailing arms to the floor in an effort to get her in a position whereby she could be carried off to her bedroom. During this process, her face somehow was scratched. The injury was noticeable. The next day at school, she told everyone that her daddy had scratched her in a fight. Luckily I had called ahead and warned the school what had happened prior to her sharing the more colorful rendition of the story.

As my daughter neared puberty, it became increasingly more challenging to contain her when she raged. Throughout these wearisome years, we stayed in close contact and accountability with a counselor and psychiatrist, also a guard against misrepresentation.

In retrospect, we did all we could do in these very difficult situations. But we did not resort to physical abuse, name calling, or other forms of verbal abuse. Consequently, whenever our daughter remembered this event and the many others in the years that followed it, she was able to focus on *her* role in what really happened and not be mentally or emotionally sidetracked by any real injustices such as verbal, emotional, or physical abuse, because they did not happen.

Choose Carefully

There are those times with my children when I must "tell it like it is." When those times come, I choose my words carefully. My voice may be forceful or sound harsh laced with frustration, but my words are not irresponsible. I do not shield my children from reality. Truth doesn't destroy, even if my children do not want to hear it.

In my California friend's phone call to discuss her latest struggles with her teen girl, she described many a parent's worse nightmares in raising a daughter. The girl was using drugs and in a romantic relationship with another girl. When the other girl broke off relationship with her, she began cutting, unable to process the trauma. Her behaviors, attitudes, and screaming rages left her parents devoid of internal resources. The mother's response was to match the daughter's behaviors: raging, name calling, and emotionally abusing.

> I do not shield my children from reality. Truth doesn't destroy, even if my children do not want to hear it.

As the girl approached age sixteen, she balked at the destruction, through abuse, that had been modeled as acceptable in the family's home. The mother's indulgence in name calling in a failed attempt to control her had only further reduced the girl's sense of responsibility to submit to her parents in what had become an unhealthy environment for the entire family. The girl was removed from the home by the Department of Human Services, put in a residential treatment facility, and eventually placed in foster care. She related to counselors and others that she had not felt safe with her parents. The tragic truth was that she was deeply loved.

Although we may not see the immediate fruit of our parenting efforts, we must choose carefully to moderate our response to emotionally charged showdowns in our homes. In so doing, we honor God behind closed doors just as fervently as we would if we lived in a televised reality show. After all, God exhorts us not to get tired of doing what is good. "At just the right time we will reap a harvest of blessing if we don't give up" (Galatians 6:9).

Reflective Prayer

Heavenly Father,

You know all the times I've failed, those times I've submitted to my own rage. I ask for Your forgiveness.

Thank you for Your gift of forgiveness. I stand before You, free of all guilt, because You have said You are "faithful and just to forgive" me of my sins and cleanse me "from all unrighteousness" (1 John 1:9 NKJV). I am fully accountable to You, no matter who or what assails me. Empower me to remember my place in the battle.

Your Word says You didn't send Jesus into the world to condemn me but rather to save me (John 3:17 NIV), so I declare there is no condemnation of me in Christ (Romans 8:1). I don't "think lightly of the riches" of Your kindness, tolerance, or patience. Instead, I respond to Your kindness with repentance (Romans 2:4 NASB). And I choose to respond to others based on who I am in You, living my life without regrets, regardless of the choices of loved ones.

The "Kingdom of God is not just a lot of talk; it is living" by Your power (1 Corinthians 4:20). "There is no one like You! For you are great, and your name is full of power" (Jeremiah 10:6). "The name of the LORD is a strong fortress"; I'm running to You. And I decree I will be safe (Proverbs 18:10)! In Jesus' Name I pray these words. Amen.

Chapter Ten

Moving from Identity to Ownership

Labels come with diagnoses. Those labels can be door closers at camps, extracurricular activities, and enrichment opportunities that deny admittance to children with special needs. They can shame and unfairly lump children into unflattering, cookie-cutter molds. Or those same labels can work for the good of the child being labeled as well as for those who need to understand and offer compassion and necessary helps.

Good labels—accurate labels based on accurate diagnosis—make it possible for children with disabilities to be understood by others and to receive their help. Those labels also give parents search terms to find a community of prevailing parents and a wealth of enlightening information. Even more importantly, good labels open the door to accommodations and services for your child, especially in academic settings. And with empathetic yet accountability based parenting, they enable children with hidden disabilities to embrace their differences and face their challenges.

Labels, Not Limits

My daughter is brilliant. It turns out those hours I spent every night with her on homework during her elementary years, working through screaming fits to get her to jump through the same hoops as her peers, was not as necessary as I thought. And it was relationship damaging for us both. Her challenges were not academic.

She remembers now how she laughed in kindergarten that her classmates were learning to sound out letters ("A: ah") when she was already speed-reading Shel Silverstein's poetry, comprehending the sophisticated humor of placing a brassiere on a camel. For her, kindergarten was difficult in other ways. It required complex tasks for her such as standing in line and interacting with others.

Finally, when she reached fifth grade, I became empowered to join her classroom teachers in the decision making over time spent on homework and classroom accommodations. I learned, as a parent of a child with special needs, that I had the right to mold expectations and requirements for my daughter in her school setting. The resources I had to use were the school system's 504 behavioral plans and IEPs. Without the labeling provided by accurate diagnosis, however, my hands would have been tied.

One challenge that comes with labeling, even when it is accurate, is over identification with the labels to the point that the label becomes the child's identity. The problem is even greater when the labeling is inaccurate. I know a woman who had a severe case of encephalitis as a child. She was selected to be part of a hospital-based study to track her development after the illness, providing her parents with expectations for her future. The assumption of the study was that every child who had contracted this illness would suffer from some degree of or even a debilitating loss of intelligence.

Unfortunately, my friend came from a highly dysfunctional family in which the parents spent more effort obtaining their next bottle of booze than they ever did on raising their children. Because of the hospital study label, my friend's mother introduced her regularly as she grew up by saying, "This is our brain-damaged daughter." The child was understandably unmotivated in school!

In spite of my friend's proven intelligence and lack of brain damage, to this day she struggles, not only with tasks like spelling but also in areas of self-esteem related to intellect. She says it is because of coasting during her academic years on the identity wrongly assigned to her by her parents. Had she been encouraged to develop according to her actual abilities, her progress would have charted differently.

This same dynamic happens more subtly when we inadvertently encourage our children to internalize their labels, accurate or not. It is important to be intentional in explaining to a child diagnosed

> It is important to be intentional in explaining to a child diagnosed with a brain chemistry condition such as ADHD, for example, that the label does not excuse less than best efforts.

with a brain chemistry condition such as ADHD, for example, that the label does not excuse less than best efforts. Empathizing with demonstrated struggles is very different than assuming a child cannot excel in predetermined ways due to a diagnosis.

The year I was trying to decide what accommodations to suggest in formation of my daughter's 504 behavior plan for school, friends recommended a local psychologist to assist in determining expectations. I went to a seminar he hosted and heard his very empathetic appeals, made on behalf of children who suffer with ADHD and are saddled with copious amounts of homework. He made numerous statements about what these children *cannot* do.

I decided against using his counsel. Instead, I chose to discover all the ways my child *could* excel and avoid false ceilings for accomplishments. I empathized with my child's struggles, but I also rejected the limiting assessments. As a result, my daughter enjoyed the sense of satisfaction gained through tackling challenges that may have been dismissed by formula due to her diagnosis.

The Challenge of Ownership

When my daughter was young, if someone were to ask her to describe herself, she might have answered with a long string of diagnostic acronyms (ADHD, OCD, and others). But those labels did not describe who she was as a person: my precious daughter! More accurately, she might have said she was a brilliant, well-read little girl who delighted in mythology, poetry, and drawing. These are the qualities I was intentional to point out to her.

What I desired during her younger years was that she achieve ownership, not identity in her diagnoses. Eventually she rejected the identity she embraced with the labels, but simultaneously she also rejected ownership. For a season, she declared nothing was wrong with her. In so doing, she also stopped taking responsibility for her own differences. This too was unhealthy.

Teaching ownership of the challenges described by labels to our children is difficult because of the negativity attached to neurological or psychiatric disabilities. The common response to these labels is shame. Some parents attempt to address the shame issue by telling their children they *can't* do certain things because of their diagnosis, offering them no culpability for their behaviors.

Designating what my children could not do was an approach I did not embrace because I believed it to be limiting. Instead, I brought them supports in the areas where they actually struggled and did not assume diagnoses defined ability. I taught them that everybody faces challenges, and certain aspects of performance in life are more difficult for them than for someone else. At the same time, I told them repeatedly, in order to fight off the negativity and shame, that other tasks are easier for them than for another. Learning how to overcome challenges, I emphasized, makes a person stronger and more capable.

> Learning how to overcome challenges, I emphasized, makes a person stronger and more capable.

Many parents become confused by the myriad of labels they encounter as their children grow. An IQ test, for example, isn't a ceiling describing one's intelligence. Instead, it is a baseline. The difference between a ceiling and a baseline is huge. In other words, a child is *at least as* intelligent as measured, which is a non-limiting perspective.

Although diagnoses and labels do not define our children, we do need to acknowledge that their challenges resulting from those diagnoses deeply affect their lives and shape them. We can strive to create a sense of normalcy for our children along with the ownership they must take of their diagnoses. One way to do so is to provide them role models—people with similar challenges who are successful and respected. Accurate portrayals give them positive, concrete images to which they can compare themselves.

The Impact of Portrayals

Most media portrayals of people with autism show them as having no emotion at all. People with schizophrenia are portrayed as dangerous. Those with bipolar are depicted as unstable and irrational. Those with ADHD are shown as lacking self-control as a result of poor parental supervision and broken homes, like the character Sid in *Toy Story*. The messages our children receive from these negative and one-dimensional media portrayals are that they are freaks, attention seekers, liars, lazy, or crazy. These messages are what children with psychiatric hidden disabilities hear more than any others about who they are. Societal stigma that rises out of inaccurate media portrayals is the biggest impediment for children and adults to owning up to mental health issues and neurological challenges.

But hope is on the horizon, as awareness increases, for the messages now sent through media. Years ago the animated television program, *Arthur*, aired an excellent series on autism to help typical children understand autistic experience. The character Penelope in *Wreck It Ralph* is the first healthy animated representation, to my knowledge, of a Tourette's syndrome-like malady that's portrayed with compassion. As mentioned earlier, the television program *Monk* typifies a brilliant detective who struggles with OCD.

Besides media, casual conversation patterns that become popular to use may also be inaccurate portrayals that cast negativity on those who struggle with hidden disabilities. When psychiatric labels are used in conversations as a joke or an insult, children with hidden disabilities are aware. Here is an example. It's common right now, when someone uses excessive profanity, to retort in response, "Do you have Tourette's or something?" My children notice, and it's not funny to them.

If parents are the only voices telling children they are okay, in the children's mind, those voices don't count. From their wounded perspective, the portrayals they receive from every other source are that they are freaks. Nobody wants to own that label.

Very few in our society openly use or enjoy racial jokes today, in contrast to fifty years ago when many people thought nothing of entertaining a good laugh at the expense of marginalized peoples. Polish jokes, popular in my childhood, fell out of vogue as Poles suffered on the world's stage. The character and bravery of Poles became enviable. I live for a day when mental health, brain chemistry, and other hidden disabilities are no longer made to be funny or a matter of shame. I look forward to a time when all of society recognizes as enviable the character and bravery of people who excel in spite of any kind of disability.

As a young man, an extended family member of mine casually quipped to an acquaintance in a passing conversation that something was "as funny as cancer." His statement was meant to imply (in what he believed was a humorous way) that the "something" wasn't funny at all. As the acquaintance walked away, my family member realized his mistake. The acquaintance's wife was actually dying of cancer. He cringed at his faux pas, sorry he had opened his mouth and used such a trendy expression with no thought about the person he was speaking with.

How many jokes are made in your children's hearing or even directly to your children about brain damage, bipolar disorder, ADHD, low IQ, dyslexia, Tourette's syndrome, autism, or any other of a host of challenges? Unfortunately, people in the general public sometimes use their growing awareness of disability labels to make more specific their cutting jokes. They do so at the expense of our children and our families, only increasing the stigma and magnifying shame.

True Identity

Identity is an important matter. We forfeit our destiny when we embrace the wrong identity. As parents of children with challenges, we are going to have a difficult time teaching our children to embrace their true identity if we fail to understand our own issues with identity. In addition, carrying the weight of the identity issues of our children, our own identities are accosted by our perceived failures as parents in raising them.

> **Identity is an important matter. We forfeit our destiny when we embrace the wrong identity.**

We may feel inadequate, constantly faced with peers whose problems seem so ridiculously minor in contrast to our own. "I just can't get Gertie to eat her peas! I know she eats other vegetables, but don't you think I should make her eat at least one bite? After all, I did prepare dinner, and her palate should be exposed to a great variety of foods!"

At other times we may feel angry inside, indignant, or filled with grief. I can recall sometimes, when my children were small, feeling overwhelmed by grief at the comparison I shouldn't but couldn't help but make between my family life and that of others. More recently, it has been difficult to rejoice about my friend's detailed description of praying with her teenaged son who is seeking God's best for his life when on some days I'm elated just to hear a polite greeting from my own son. I know my son is learning and growing and also making great strides. But when my guard is down and if I'm not careful, I can feel like "less" and stumble in the face of the mountain of temptation to allow feelings to define me and my worth as a mother.

The good reputation you may once have enjoyed as the "go to" mom for wise counsel on child rearing may have all but disappeared after birthing your child with hidden disabilities. The entire family dynamic is changed by the addition of a child who struggles with behavioral problems. Other parents see your child acting out; in your home, you face the loss of household peace. You feel inadequate as a parent, and other parents no longer see you in the same positive light. It's a double whammy against your identity.

Losing our previous roles is a necessary loss to gain what is next. We are given the opportunity to evaluate exactly where our identity is rooted in the first place.

Is our identity in being a responsible parent of excellence represented by stellar children? Is our identity wrapped up in the esteem we enjoy from others? Is our identity tied to spiritual involvements at church or in community activities? If any of these questions are a yes for you, the toll of raising children with special needs will be great, and your perception of your identity will fluctuate according to successes and failures.

In contrast, what does God say about who you are? When God defines who you are, it is immutable. Your identity rests and remains constant in your relationship to Him. You are loved unconditionally (1 John 4:8). You have God's wisdom (1 Corinthians 1:30). You are a new creation, made in His likeness (2 Corinthians 5:17 ESV). You live and move through this life for the praise of His glory (Ephesians 1:12 NIV). Your identity is cemented and secure in the truth of God's Word.

The book of Ezra tells a story of Israelites returning to their homeland from Babylonian exile. Ezra reestablished the Temple in Jerusalem and scriptural worship. Birthright determined those who were to serve in the Temple as priests, but while in captivity some priests had taken on the names of their wives, no longer considering their heritage represented by their ancestral names of significance in a foreign land with no Temple for their worship. Losing their lineal names, however, meant losing their own identities; they couldn't be located in ancestral records. By forsaking their true identities, they had forfeited their destinies as priests of the Temple.

This story contained good news as well. The identities of the priests, and thus their destinies, were recoverable after all. Scripture explains that finding their true identities and stepping into their destinies could be accomplished by seeking God for confirmation of who they were (Ezra 2:62–63).

Our true identities are found in who God says we are. The same is true for our children. The greatest truth about my daughter is not her depression, her outbursts, or her anxiety. It is instead everything God created her to be. The greatest truth about my son is not his failing grades. Over time, he will find effective strategies for academics. The greatest truth about him is the awesome young man he is now and the incredible man of God he is destined to become. Likewise, the greatest truth about my identity is not found in my service, performance, or successes. My identity is found in who I am as a daughter of the Most High. And I am that, no matter what frustrations I conquer or fail to conquer. Who I am is unchangeable.

Meaningful Accommodations

I don't let my children get away with assertions like, "I can't do math." Research shows that children with Tourette's syndrome do typically struggle with math. But "struggling" does not equate to "can't." With that said, there may be some things children with hidden disabilities genuinely can't do, just like there are for children with physical disabilities. They can, however, invent work-arounds for those limitations. Teaching our children to self-accommodate is one of the most helpful interventions we can offer them.

Brainstorming self-accommodations happens when children take ownership of their differences. And ownership happens when there is accountability. In contrast, when parents convey disabilities or disadvantages as defining their children (identity), they hold them back by not requiring the accountability the children need to develop personal responsibility. The way

> Teaching our children to self-accommodate is one of the most helpful interventions we can offer them.

to hold a child with hidden disabilities accountable is by offering concomitant empathy. There is no pre-determined ceiling. Who is to say what any of them may accomplish?

As I shared previously, my daughter is sensory sensitive. When she was younger, she would yell and scream at the family to shut up because she couldn't think. At times even the typical noise level in a house of five people would send her flying into a rage. If my husband and I had allowed her diagnosis of Sensory Integration Disorder to define who she was, we would have accepted her screams and chalked it up to her "pathology." We would have defended her behaviors as part of her genetic constitution. Instead, we taught ownership, requiring accountability, while offering empathy.

She was truly sensory sensitive. Sensitivity was not her fault, and she could not help being sensitive. We communicated our understanding of her dilemma. But, we added, she could, with great effort, control how she behaved when accosted by noises. Her sensitivity was *her* problem. Because we loved our daughter and were aware of her challenges, we responded to her self-advocacy of alerting us when she was especially sensitive.

In addition to teaching her ownership, empathy, and accountability, we equipped her with strategies she could employ when troubled by noises. Equipping was critical, we told her, because not everyone would accommodate her throughout her lifetime. She would have to become responsible for accommodating herself. She learned, and to this day, she sports noise-cancelling headphones to control auditory input.

Others did not always understand the accommodations my children needed. As you might imagine, I received many a judgmental glare when allowing my daughter to wear her headphones during a church service. Part of the empathy piece is allowing our children to self-accommodate. They know their limits.

My daughter's insistence on going barefoot outdoors as a child was frowned upon by some onlookers as well. But being barefoot, she learned, was a way for her to receive input through her feet that was body/mind centering, making her feel calmer. Additionally, my husband and I created a waist belt purse for her to carry that held sensory, squeezable, textured toys to calm her during boring waits. My daughter's teacher was not pleased when I insisted she take this bag on the symphony field trip, but my daughter needed it to self-accommodate when the "wait" became too long. The goal, always, was to empower her while also holding her accountable.

Honest recognition and appropriate ownership of diagnoses, accountability, empathy, and accommodation strategies lead our children to an adulthood of self-awareness and personal responsibility. The opposite also is true. Accountability without empathy and acknowledgement of our children's very real struggles will eventually convince them that they truly *are* the embodiment of the undesired behaviors. They will internalize their behaviors to believe they *are* lazy, *are* lacking, *are* rebellious, and so on.

Behaviors, failures, accomplishments, or achievements do not form the foundation of our children's identity or ours. According to the Word of God (Ephesians 2:10), we are God's masterpieces!

Reflective Prayer

Heavenly Father,

I offer up to You my identity. I give to You what other people think about me. And I ask that You reaffirm for me who I am in You, just as You reestablished the identities and destinies of the priests, as recorded in Ezra 2.

In You I am light in this world, and the light that shines from me glorifies You (Matthew 5:16 NIV). I lay my treasures up in heaven, where they can't be destroyed by disappointments or by my child's problems down here on the earth (Matthew 6:20 ESV).

I didn't choose You; rather You chose me and ordained that I bear fruit, fruit that will remain (John 15:16 KJV). Based on the truth of Your Word, I decree in Jesus' name that my life is valuable and will bear lasting fruit as I labor raising my children.

I am God's gift to Jesus (John 17:9–10). Help me to embrace this true identity. I declare that "no power in the sky above or in the earth below—indeed, nothing in all creation will ever be able to separate" me or my child "from the love of God that is revealed in Christ Jesus" my Lord (Romans 8:39). In Jesus' name I pray these words. Amen.

Chapter Eleven

The Triumvirate Mental Health Model

Theologians long have maintained the interconnectedness of body, soul, and spirit. This three-part view of human nature, widely accepted among Christians, asserts that mankind *is* spirit, *possesses* a soul, and *lives* in a body. The thought is echoed in the apostle Paul's prayer, "Now may the God of peace make you holy in every way, and may your whole spirit and soul and body be kept blameless until our Lord Jesus Christ comes again" (1 Thessalonians 5:23). What are the implications of the three-part nature of humanity for mental health?

The term *triumvirate* in this chapter refers to the three powerful entities that exist in relation to one another: spirit, soul, and body. The *triumvirate mental health model*, a phrase I am coining for my own purposes, acknowledges the interplay of the three as it relates to mental health. In my mind, the biggest implication of this model for those of us with children who face mental health challenges is this: mental illness may *originate* from the material part of our being, which is the brain, or from the immaterial parts, which are the soul and the spirit; and from its origination, it may *progress* to involve other parts. Treatment, therefore, requires more than a single approach.

The Chicken or the Egg?

"Which came first?" is thought to be a critical question when exploring the origin of a mental health disorder. Is a person's mental health challenge related to a physiological brain issue? Does it stem from an emotional issue? (I can't tell you how many times my daughter has been referred to as a child having an "emotional" problem!) Is a person's mental health challenge rooted in a spiritual issue? Or is it related to all three?

I am proposing here that "which came first" doesn't matter. All three aspects of a person's being are involved in mental health. Without a holistic, interventive response that encompasses the entirety of a person's nature—body, soul, and spirit—"wholeness" with respect to mental health is elusive. Differing professionals are needed to address therapeutically each of the three components of our human nature as it impacts mental health.

> **Without a holistic, interventive response that encompasses the entirety of a person's nature—body, soul, and spirit—"wholeness" with respect to mental health is elusive.**

Treatment for the "Body"

Medical science professionals focus on the truth that mental health can have a physical, neurological origin. The brain's chemical bath facilitates synapse message sharing among the neurons that comprise the brain. Whether in the reception of those chemicals or in their production, imbalances create mental health symptoms, some more severe and noticeable but not any less real than others. Brain dysfunction is known to cause a wide range of symptoms, including panic attacks, depression, seizures, obsessions, distractibility, confusion, memory loss, irrationality, irritability, volatility, delusions, tics, and a host of others.

Science textbooks, neurobiological research, and psychiatrists communicate the message clearly: there is a medical, biological, physiological basis for mental health disorders. Psychiatric doctors are one of the medical professionals most qualified to prescribe medication to "level the playing field," or intervene to create as close as possible a return to balanced chemistry and symptom relief for those with mental illness.

Simple depression with no situational antecedent is a good example of a physically based mental health condition. Quick treatment with an antidepressant can bring substantial relief, or at the very least return the sufferer to a more tolerable state. It's important to note here, however, that physically based mental health conditions may be treatable with medications but not curable, at least at this point in time.

Psychiatrists these days typically recognize the critical role behavioral psychologists and counselors fulfill in exploring patients' choices, thinking, and emotions that impact mental health outcomes, even when the mental health challenge has originated in the physiology of the brain. More recently many psychiatrists also recognize the critical role the spiritual plays in recovery, as evidenced most blatantly by politically correct, universalist spiritual components such as meditation, spirit guides, and the addressing of existential concerns that are offered as complementary interventions in many psychiatric treatment institutions. Even though psychiatrists are trained and qualified specifically to treat the "body" component, most acknowledge the relevance and benefits of patients addressing the immaterial parts of their nature as well—the soul and the spirit.

Treatment for the "Soul"

The soul encompasses both the conscious and unconscious mind, forming personality. A person's thinking, reasoning, memories, attitudes, beliefs, will, emotions, and choices are in the realm of the soul. It is easy for most of us to see how mental illness can originate from the soul as well as from the body.

Psychologists and counselors are the professionals trained to address mental health conditions that emerge from the soul. Those that offer counseling services, whether specifically Christian or not, address the life experiences of patients that can cause woundedness of the soul, which can have profound impact on mental health. Counseling is an important component of an individual's full recovery from the devastation of the soul caused not only by poor personal choices but also the poor choices of others.

> Counseling is an important component of an individual's full recovery from the devastation of the soul caused not only by poor personal choices but also the poor choices of others.

Mental illness that stems from the soul may be temporary in nature and respond well to quality counseling. Examples of short-term mental health issues that may be resolvable through counseling include situational-based depression and some anxiety disorders. An anxiety disorder that surfaces from patient experiences, such as a severe fear of dogs after being attacked by a pack of canines as a child, is an example of an anxiety disorder that is soul based.

Sometimes a psychologist or counselor may refer a patient to a psychiatrist even though the diagnosed mental health issue originated in the soul. There is benefit, for example, to treating situational, emotionally based depression in part with drugs to protect the brain from the flood of negative neurochemical mixes resultant from depression. The rationale behind the medicinal treatment is brain preservation, not just lessening the patient's suffering.

Psychologists and counselors also understand that not all mental illness is soul based, even though a patient may seek intervention through them first. They acknowledge that not all who suffer from mental illness do so because of woundedness in their histories or because of their own poor life choices. The wise ones refer these patients to psychiatrists to address underlying physiological brain chemistry problems with medications or other treatment modalities that target brain cells. Counseling is still highly beneficial, however, because issues of the soul become relevant as patients grapple with the impact of their neurology on relationships and daily functioning. Additionally, counseling can impart critical coping skills.

As an example, my daughter is currently seeing a counselor to help her navigate the transition from adolescence to adulthood, a transition complicated by her neurology. Although her mental health struggles do not originate from the soul, her attitudes, beliefs, reasoning, and choices affect her ability to progress toward independence. Counseling alone, however, cannot "cure," or heal permanently, the underlying neurological, mental health disorder.

Treatment for the "Spirit"

Increasingly mental health professionals are acknowledging the role of the spiritual in mental health treatment. Many psychiatric institutions offer optional spiritual tracks as part of treatment plans that are not specific to any one religion. To many, this approach seems innocuous enough; however, I believe spiritual practices in the context of mental health treatment that are apart from the gospel of Jesus Christ open doors in one's spirit to the wrong spirit.

While researching residential treatment facilities covered by my family's insurance plan, I discovered a program that advertised nights in a sweat lodge. In this lodge, participants could seek their own personal "spirit guide" to assist them in the recovery process. Like the unrighteous trades made with the witch doctors of Indonesia described in chapter 5, I believe invitations to any spirit other than to the Holy Spirit are incredibly dangerous, even when the short-term benefit appears positive.

Christian sources are the only providers of spiritual treatment that I personally can acknowledge as beneficial in the long term. Traditional churches offer spiritual counseling, with first priority hopefully placed on explaining salvation through Jesus Christ accompanied by inner transformation. Christian counseling aids clients by helping them align thinking and behaviors with scriptural mandates and principles. The crossover benefits of Christian counseling between treatment of the soul and treatment of the spirit are great. As has already been stated, however, counseling alone does not cure a biologically based mental health disorder.

Charismatic churches and groups address needs of the human spirit in the same ways as traditional churches; however, they may also offer spiritual treatment modalities that do not cross over into treatment of the soul to the same extent as those employed by traditional churches. Charismatic treatment approaches emphasize the role of negative spiritual entities, or demons, in mental health and disease processes. These approaches are grounded in the connection between demonization and illness as seen in Scripture (see Luke 13:10–16 and Matthew 17:15–18 as examples).

I do not believe that all illness, mental health or otherwise, is spiritual in origin (beyond the fallen condition of mankind as recorded in the Scriptures). I do, however, believe that any affliction that causes suffering may be a direct result of demonic involvement. When a mental health disorder is the result of demonization, deliverance can actually bring healing that is both neurological as well as spiritual. Deliverances and the resultant healings are prevalent throughout the ministry of Jesus.

I have heard many firsthand, hair-raising stories from the mission field, and yes, even from here in the States, that support the notion that God is still at work in both deliverance ministries and miraculous healings. Like the many leaders who share the stories of these miraculous happenings overseas, I believe American Christians would see an increase in healing of all types in our contemporary churches today if believers were more attuned to the need to practice deliverance as a normal auxiliary to discipleship, not just in the treatment of mental health.

I know a Christian psychologist who treated a 14-year-old girl who'd suffered a head injury from an automobile accident. As a result of the severe head trauma, the girl began to suffer from nightmares, migraines, anger, depression, and anxiety. Her grades slipped down from honor roll to almost all F's. She fought in school and cursed her mother with regularity. Another psychologist, a psychiatrist, and a neurologist had all chipped in their diagnostic opinions, labeling her with a personality disorder, bipolar disorder, and an intermittent anger disorder.

This girl had been raised in a Christian home and was a believer. The moment my Christian psychologist friend took a look into her eyes, she discerned the girl needed deliverance, despite the mental health reports that detailed the physical head trauma. The accident had changed the girl's entire behavior, which is not uncommon with head injuries. But this psychologist believed in holistic treatment, and so she sought the Lord to understand the *true* origin of the illness. She did not make assumptions regarding the cause of symptoms.

The mother of the girl was not familiar with deliverance except horrid stories of demon possession from movies. She was not readily open to the suggestion of deliverance; however, she was desperate. So when the psychologist suggested a possible need for deliverance, the mother gave the required consent.

The psychologist proceeded by offering both biblically based "soul counsel" and prayer ministry to the girl for several weeks. On one occasion in response to the soul counsel, the young girl began to make strange sounds and manifest as a snake, slipping from her chair and crawling on her belly. Even though the girl and the psychologist were in the middle of a counseling session, the psychologist immediately stopped the session and began to command the demonic entities to loose the girl and let her go on the authority of the blood of Jesus, calling out bitterness, anger, resentment, unforgiveness, hopelessness, suicide, and so on.

After a while, the girl began to cough loudly, spitting up what the psychologist described as "a green, yucky substance." Eventually the girl crawled up off the floor and sat down in her chair. Her eyes became clear, and she was ready to resume the session. Although she was drained of all strength, both she and the psychologist realized she had just experienced deliverance. Something had changed.

Within a few weeks, the girl no longer exhibited any sign of head trauma. She had been delivered of demons and healed neurologically at the same time she was also being counseled by the Christian psychologist. Over the next two years, this girl raised her grades back to A's, once again showed respect to her parents, completed high school, and was accepted into a prestigious college.

This story demonstrates an important point for Christian psychologists and counselors as well as their patients. Deliverance ministry is a powerful tool for those who choose to become prepared to treat the spirit of mankind and not just the soul and body. In the same breath, I also want to make clear that deliverance is not a broad spectrum, silver bullet that cures all ailments, regardless of cause. Suggesting deliverance is a "cure all" can be paramount to spiritual abuse.

Christians who are trained in deliverance ministry confront root sins believed to open spiritual doors to the demonic. These root sins include internal sins such as bitterness or unforgiveness as well as behavioral sins committed by choice such as adultery and pornography usage. In addition to confronting root sins, Christians trained in deliverance may pray with a sufferer through generational repentance, following the lead of Old Testament prophets who acknowledged the sins of their forefathers during realignment with the plans and purposes of God. They also may pray to break curses. Renunciation of secret societies such as the Freemason organization is deemed important because some oaths taken by ancestral adherents actually include a curse on the mental and physical health of progeny if the oath is broken.

Deliverance can bring healing to a mental health condition that originated in the spirit. If the mental health condition originated in the soul or the body, deliverance alone, however, may not necessarily cure the problem. God, of course, is not limited to healing conditions caused by demonization. He is able to heal body, soul, and spirit regardless of root causes.

The Case for Holistic, Interventive Response

Mental illness may begin with any one of the three parts of mankind: body, soul, or spirit. But due to the interconnectedness of each part, a mental illness originating in one part typically involves the other parts as well over time. Without a holistic, interventive response that encompasses the entirety of a person's nature, complete recovery or even marked improvement from mental illness is less probable.

When a mental illness begins with neurology, brain chemistry leaves the sufferer more susceptible to behaviors such as rage, isolation, and irrational thinking that contribute to rejection by others. Resultant emotional impact, when not processed properly, may create soul issues. Believing the lies of Satan, self-pity, unforgiveness, and bitterness may open doors in the spirit to demonic entities attracted to negative, destructive emotiveness. This example shows that when an initial illness of the body goes untreated, mental health problems potentially follow that involve also the person's soul and spirit.

When the origin of a mental health challenge is the soul, prolonged and untreated mental illness can create an unhealthy, damaging bath of neurochemicals that damage the brain. Behaviors and attitudes stemming from the soul, when joined by a body-based mental health issue, may subsequently open the spirit to demonic oppression. In this example, soul first and then body and spirit are involved in the malady.

The final example is the one perhaps least understood and potentially the most dangerous. It is possible for a person with no neurological issues or soul-based dysfunction to open the self intentionally or otherwise to demonic influence that can also contribute to mental health issues. In India, for example, worshipers intentionally invite the spirits of Hindu gods to inhabit their bodies. We here in the States mimic invitations to the demonic through our own innocent practice of yoga, watered down to asana exercises, which are the positions adopted in performing yoga but nonetheless a series of postures anciently designed to invite the spirits of Hindu gods.

The term *yoga* is a Sanskrit word meaning "to yoke" or "to unite." The science of yoga is fascinating, and its practice is being linked to many objective health benefits verifiable by extensive scientific research. Perhaps the positive benefits of stretching, relaxation, exercise, centering, and mindfulness could be achieved through a methodology other than the practice of yoga. Unfortunately, separation of the physical benefits of yoga practice from the spiritual significance may not be possible. This is an opinion I share with the Hindu American Foundation, which asserts that Hinduism cannot be delinked from the practice of Yoga[20]. Additionally, in this country and elsewhere, involvement with witchcraft, Ouija boards, tarot cards, astrology, or other overt demonic invitations may be antecedents to spiritually rooted mental health or a myriad of other kinds of personal problems later.

The demonic influences that are possible through such seemingly harmless activities may inspire rage, lust, addictions, and fear as well as other negative lures that attract destructive behaviors. Soul involvement follows. And with soul involvement, mental health challenges shift brain chemistry that can damage cells over time. Here, as in the previous examples, the mental health challenge is a combination of the involvement of spirit, soul, and body.

It is important to restate here that the downward spiral of mental health can begin from any of the three component parts of mankind and incorporate the other two parts if progression is left unchecked and untreated. For this reason, it is imperative that treatment for an observed mental condition be as early as possible and holistic: addressing body, soul, and spirit.

Counseling for issues of the soul can cure a strictly soul-rooted mental health problem. And medication, when needed for brain chemistry protection and to lessen suffering, can bring relief to mental illness in the body but not cure body-, soul-, or spirit-based mental health challenges. Deliverance can bring a complete cure for a mental health disorder only when the problem is strictly spiritual in origin, which may include a spiritually induced physical problem. In other words, a triumvirate mental health model that acknowledges the powerful role of component parts of human nature in mental illness progression explains why treatment modalities addressing only one piece are less likely to resolve mental illness.

The Christian church for the most part understands body, soul, and spirit theology, which describes the tripartite nature of mankind. But does the American church's model for addressing mental health conditions and Christian behaviors toward those who struggle with mental illness adequately reflect that understanding?

Reflective Prayer

Heavenly Father,

You are the God of peace, wholeness, and holiness. Make my child and me holy in every way: in our bodies, spirits, and souls. Keep us blameless (1 Thessalonians 5:23). Did You not say that "those who err in mind will know the truth" and "those who criticize will accept instruction" (Isaiah 29:24 NASB)? "The mind set on the Spirit is life and peace" (Romans 8:6 NASB). So renew my child in the spirit of his/her mind, I ask You in Jesus' name (Ephesians 4:23 KJV).

I decree that Your peace, "which surpasses all comprehension, will guard" my child's heart and mind in Christ Jesus (Philippians 4:7 NASB). Please smile upon my child when he/she is discouraged (Job 29:24). Teach my child to acclaim You, that he/she might walk in the light of Your presence (Psalm 89:15 NIV). In Jesus' name I pray these words. Amen.

Chapter Twelve

The Church and Mental Health

Imagine with me a world in which all clergy and Christian counselors offer a holistic approach in the treatment of those who come to them to seek relief with mental health symptoms. Such broad thinking sets the tone and attitudes of church congregations for how to respond to those they encounter within the church who struggle with mental health issues. Equipped with an informed and compassionate perspective on mental illness, churches are safe and accommodating environments for all adults and children alike.

The reality is quite different. Not all clergy and counselors are as insightful. Most churches are not equipped to be safe and compassionate environments. As a result, those with mental health conditions feel they must "go underground" to deflect the judgments made against them. Because they know the truth through experience, they reject the notion, made popular from the pulpit, that prayer and Bible study alone can free them from their mental health struggles. And in many cases, the insistence from well-meaning others that these spiritual practices alone can set them free drives them away from the church.

Where's Waldo?

The prevalence of mental illnesses is much higher than most churches recognize, so the need to address the concern is not high on their list. One reason is that the unsafe environment at church for disclosure makes it difficult for those who struggle to share their condition or make their needs known. Mental illness is not a topic that most people, beyond the rare celebrity who

> The prevalence of mental illnesses is much higher than most churches recognize, so the need to address the concern is not high on their list.

feels assured of social acceptability due to fame, feel free to discuss openly. Instead, average persons struggling with mental health issues tend to hide. After a
time of trial and failure to fit in, they either abandon church, and sometimes God
with it, or sit in the congregation and conceal their secret.

Mental health sufferers are painfully aware that the label "mentally ill" con-
jures images of today's popular reality show oddities that eat sticks of deodorant
as their "strange addiction." Or images of "those kind of people" in the news and
how they shot up a classroom full of children or did other harm to society. These
images prevail, in spite of the fact that people who struggle with mental health are
far more likely to be victims of crime than perpetrators. Sensational portrayals
sell and twist reality, while the sufferers hide, afraid to let their needs be known.

Average churchgoers seem oblivious to the fact that people who struggle with
mental illnesses are all around them as members of the congregation, members
of the staff, and even close friends. The lack of awareness reminds me of a naive
assumption from my childhood. I used to believe drug abusers wore black trench
coats and hawked their wares by grasping their lapels and exposing contraband.
Because of this misconception, I didn't recognize that real drug users very well
could be in my inner circle of friends or theoretically even be my own siblings.

Those that struggle with mental health challenges are far more common than
most people suspect, although not often overtly obvious. According to mental
health statistics, over a third of Americans could meet criteria for diagnosis of one
or more of the common types of mental disorder in any given year[21]. An astound-
ing number. Worth reflection.

The number alone of people with mental health challenges means they are
not an expendable proportion of the population that clergy and churches can
afford to alienate or to ignore their needs. Statistically, Waldo is in every pew.

In Search of a Holistic, Shame-Free Approach

Traditional denominational churches typically are sensitive to the needs of
parishioners in relation to their memories, reasoning, beliefs, attitudes, and choices as far as how those soul-impacting elements contribute to their mental health.
Many employ wise spiritual principles in counseling their people that touch on
elements of the spirit, such as regeneration through submission of one's will to
God and transformation through the indwelling presence of the Holy Spirit.

Many more churches, however, avoid or intentionally ignore the very real and
possible role of the demonic realm as a causative agent for mental illness. They

fail to go beyond the simple acknowledgment of "evil" motivation as a reason for behavioral or attitudinal sin. Admittedly, under emphasis may be the lesser of two evils, the greater being an overemphasis on the possible role of the demonic.

In some mainline denominations, accepted theological constructs relegate the Bible's weapons for spiritual warfare to the dusty closet labeled "archaic" or to the realm of "foreign missions." The result is that those parishioners suffering from the effects of curses or direct demonic oppression receive little to no help from them. Even overt demonic manifestations such as night visitations by spirits, when disclosed by one suffering, are dismissed by church leaders as evidence of simple mental instability. In truth, such apparitions could be seen as obvious direction for needed ministry.

For most churches that ignore the demonic realm, the decision is less of an oversight and more of a theological position. But it's entirely possible the problem in some is related to lack of adequate preparation for the needed ministry. Such preparation could include equipping and training in understanding spiritual authority and learning a "casual" deliverance model. By casual model, I mean one that is offered without fanfare. If we think of demons that trouble individuals like potentially harmful bacteria on dirty hands, a casual approach would be to offer the blood of Jesus regularly for cleansing of the spirit much like one would casually use soap and water on hands that need cleansing.

This analogy is somewhat simplified. Some bacteria are fairly powerless and easy to wash away. Some are highly pathogenic and put up quite a fight once infecting an individual. The same is true with demons. Churches that fail to acknowledge or address the role of demons in spiritual pathology or to practice spiritual warfare may unintentionally leave sufferers in their bondage.

Far more obvious to those suffering from mental health problems than the omission of spiritual warfare to help their condition is the lack of churches to address one of the three aspects of the triumvirate model of health, the "body" origin of mental illness. Some pastors denigrate the need for depression medication in swipes made from the pulpit, suggesting antidepressants are "cop-outs." By talking down medication and acknowledging exclusively the "soul" origin of mental illness, these leaders deem those around them who suffer from mental health challenges to be simply "character defective."

This characterization is frequently made after years of spiritually principled counseling have not resolved a mental health issue. When all known church-based help is exhausted, leaders who are not equipped to do more resort to peddled "spiritual" advice. They purport God-honoring behavioral and attitudinal changes are the only cures, insinuating guilt, as though the mentally ill have resisted the counsel offered. Shame is added to the challenges of the sufferers.

With respect to ignoring or discouraging the viable role of psychiatry in the treatment of physically based mental illness, charismatic churches fare no better than traditional denominations. These "Spirit-filled churches" tend to emphasize the possible "spirit" causes of mental illness over the "soul" causes and the "body" causes. A parishioner's disclosure of a mental health diagnosis can lead to a one-way ticket to the church's Deliverance Team.

> "Spirit-filled churches" tend to emphasize the possible "spirit" causes of mental illness over the "soul" causes and the "body" causes.

Occasionally in charismatic churches, complete healing of a mental health disorder occurs through deliverance. When healing does not happen, however, spiritual practitioners in these churches sometimes make unwarranted assumptions that can harm the sufferers. Those assumptions include demonic doors remaining open through sin, unaddressed "soul ties" to negative figures in a sufferer's history, rebellion, "un-thorough repentance" for past sins, and more.

Although charismatic churches may offer counseling to cover concerns of the soul, some make another mistake that is the same mistake as traditional churches. They assume *all* those with mental health struggles possess a certain amount of personal culpability for their own suffering. This assumption in turn lessens their compassion. When culpability for mental illness is assumed, the occasional pulpit reference to mental illness is rarely empathetic. The parishioners who suffer with mental health challenges then pick up, through inference, the judgments being made about their personal, emotional, and spiritual condition. Church is no longer seen as a safe and welcoming place. Instead it becomes an unsafe environment for disclosure of their mental health struggles.

Safe Environments

Today's increased awareness of making the church and community a safe environment falls far short of the need, but it is at least a step in the right direction. Safe environments play therapeutic and supportive roles for those battling with mental illness in their own lives or in the lives of their children. It is not churches, as we might wish, but educational institutions that are leading the way, aggressively seeking to become safe environments. Thanks in part to both national mandate and the caring hearts of school professionals, students can now make their needs known.

My son was fortunate to have a safe environment during his elementary years in school. In the second grade, he had a head-shaking tic. I taught him to self-advocate so that his teacher did not mistake his tic for saying no and appearing defiant. The teacher embraced my son's disclosure, and he was not misjudged. More importantly, she made a safe environment for him to learn and grow.

Those diagnosed with mental illness, although protected by disability laws, may not fare as well in the workplace as in a school environment. Workplaces can be less accommodating and unsafe. My young adult daughter told her trainer at a new job about her anxiety disorder that caused her tics to increase with nervousness. The trainer, unfortunately, used the information against her. She made fun of my daughter's tics. On one occasion when my daughter was with her in an elevator, this trainer jumped up and down in the elevator to get it to shake. When the elevator door opened, she blocked my daughter's exit. As she did so, she informed my daughter that her anxiety was "all in her head" and could be cured by such antics.

No place, in my mind, is the absence of a safe environment for those suffering with mental health challenges more disturbing and damaging to the mentally ill than in the church, among Christians. Church is the *one* place where sufferers need to be free to disclose their struggles without judgment or pronouncements of ill informed, simplistic paths forward for healing.

Churches, admittedly, are beginning to understand the message of inclusion, especially with respect to children suffering with hidden disabilities. And they are beginning to understand the need to minister to the entire family, not just the family member with a disability. The Web site Church4EveryChild[22] is dedicated to helping churches address the needs of children with mental illness, trauma, or developmental disabilities as well as their entire families. Key Ministry[23] is an organization that provides free resources to those interested in creating a ministry environment that is inclusive, equipping churches to reach families affected by disability.

Some churches have begun to reach out to struggling families by providing respite care. Respite care offers temporary relief for parents by arranging short-term free or subsidized child-care services. This critically important ministry enables parents to recharge spiritually, emotionally, and physically.

Avoiding Insulting or Simplistic Paths Forward

Church advances in inclusion and ministering to the whole family are commendable. More, much more is still needed, including interventions that help without hurting.

Church-based spiritual and emotional counseling is a valid and much needed piece of intervention. Most churches offer this counseling or at least give referrals. Such counseling is not just a temporary need for the resolution of mental health challenges. Instead, for many, it must be ongoing, even lifelong, to support the coping skills of individuals who struggle with neurologically based mental illness. The need for continuing counseling does *not*, however, denote a lack of character or spiritual maturity. This judgment is both simplistic and insulting.

Though counseling may offer profound help to the sufferers, it does not cure afflictions of the spirit that involve demonization, afflictions that can result independent of culpability. Also and again, counseling does not cure physical brain chemistry mental health issues.

In churches where demonization is understood as a root cause for some mental illnesses, clergy and lay leaders would do well not to "single out" those with mental illness for ministering deliverance prayers to ensure demonic oppression is minimized. Instead, a deliverance ministry can be offered as a normal, preventative measure as a part of discipleship of all believers. A deliverance ministry is merely a prayer ministry using leaders trained in spiritual authority to ensure Christians are free from spiritual bondages. It can be presented as an ongoing resource for all who come to a church rather than as a Hollywood inspired, dramatic, fringe event for particularly sinful or "crazed" people.

In one church I attended, all new believers were invited to participate in a weekend "healing" journey during which biblical counseling and deliverance was offered to all equally. Because of this carefully reasoned approach, every member of the congregation at that church could benefit from limiting the effects of demonic oppression, not just those who suffered from mental health challenges. The inclusive approach was equipping, not insulting.

Churches would do well to support rather than denigrate treatment modalities outside of the walls of the church that address each of the component parts of mankind where mental

> Churches would do well to support rather than denigrate treatment modalities outside of the walls of the church that address each of the component parts of mankind where mental illness may originate.

illness may originate. Going forward, the merits of psychiatry, including under some circumstances brain chemistry medication, could be validated from the pulpits of churches. It is possible and doable for churches that desire to reach all people to correct the misdirection of the past, which offered simplistic explanations for mental illness. And it is possible and doable for churches to halt the unrighteous judgments by the uninformed, both in the congregations and the leadership, against those who suffer enough already.

Some churches are already well on their way to correcting these wrongs. Not only have they incorporated special needs ministries into their offerings, but they also are increasing in awareness that disabilities encompass more than overt mobility or intellectual handicaps. They are less concerned about labels and the judgments that accompany them. And they are more concerned about creating whatever environment is needed for inclusion of *everyone* in the mutual goal we all share of becoming more like Christ.

Accommodations

When clergy and churches intentionally admit and shed their incomplete understanding of the origins of mental illness and with it the judgments, sufferers become free to disclose their struggles. A safe environment, then, leads to an accommodating environment. Accommodations can be made because "need" can be expressed in an atmosphere of acceptance, free from shame or judgment. And maybe even more importantly for the hearts of all involved, accommodations can be made to open the church to share God's love to all people, regardless of abilities or disabilities.

I've seen it happen. When churches choose to become accepting environments and needs are made known by newcomers, accommodations are made responsively, without a second thought. The needed accommodations for those with mental health challenges become part of a total caring environment of the church. They are added to the care already extended to those with vision, hearing, and physical mobility challenges.

My family attended a mega-church for over a decade but ended up having to leave it. My son's loud, vocal tics were not appropriate during service in the sanctuary, but we faced a situation out of our control. The children were not dismissed for classes until a third of the way through the main service. In an attempt to deal with the uncomfortable interruptions, I obtained permission from the head of the children's department for my son to be in the children's sanctuary during that time. But every week, without fail, one of the volunteer teens that rotated through the children's program would make my son find me in a sanctuary of ten thousand people because he wasn't "allowed back there yet." My son repeatedly explained his dilemma, but the teen volunteers always had to hear it from me personally. So every Sunday, I watched my son wilt a little more.

Finally we left our large worship center with its elaborate children's program for a tiny church with four white walls and twelve children in my son's class. We were able to tell his new teacher *one* time about my son's disability and never mention it again. The smaller church accommodated my son and became a safe environment.

Although accommodations may require intentionality, the choice to provide a safe environment enables accommodations to happen quite naturally through empathy, understanding, and genuine concern. This truth plays out in other environments. For example, when I enjoy hosting the company of an elderly couple on a social outing, I accommodate their unique needs. I exercise wisdom by ensuring my elderly friends are not placed in a situation where they must stand for long periods of time. I suggest meals in a timely manner. I confirm that restrooms are nearby and make sure they know the locations. I lovingly protect my elderly guests from situations that would highlight their frailties. Such accommodations are a natural part of sensitive and caring relationships. They can happen in the church as well.

My friend shared a story of children modeling "natural" accommodations as an example to the adults. Once she was part of a team providing care for children in the children's area of the church as their parents attended a workshop on raising children. She noted how the leader of the care team was discerning in how she grouped children at the tables of six. It was in this context she experienced an example of several children naturally accommodating a child with autism who was struggling to fit in and do the craft activities.

At one point during a craft activity, when my friend's face expressed shock at the child with autism's behavior of taking things from the other children at the table, one little girl touched her arm and said, "It's okay. He's just like that. We don't get upset about it. We're used to it." My friend was astounded by the wisdom of that child and the way the other children also accommodated so naturally, hardly even taking notice.

In a similar way, when churches become accepting environments for those who struggle with brain disorders, the particulars of the accommodations can be discerned both through empathy and constructive conversations with those who feel free to self-advocate. A man who suffers with seizures, for example, would not be selected to drive the church bus to camp. That decision is not dishonoring; it's wisdom. Just as guardrails ensure freedom for motorists to proceed with confidence, transparent honesty between church leaders and parishioners promotes safety.

The same kind of discernment afforded to the man who suffers with seizures can be used with those who have mental health challenges. A woman who expresses that she suffers from bipolar disorder, for example, may be better suited to co-lead rather than solo lead a regular, long-term church gathering. If and when her chemistry shifts, someone can be there to take the helm for a few weeks without crisis until the tide turns. The accommodation is discreet, pre-arranged, and implemented without communicating a sense of failure and shame or fall from esteem. The result of loving discernment and thoughtful accommodation is full integration of those with mental health issues into the life of the church—with care not to showcase anyone's deficits.

Every congregation can listen and respond to the needs of parents whose children require extra consideration, not just mega-churches with official special needs ministries. Flexibility and sensitivity are the key components, not large budgets and expertise. If you are the parent of a child with hidden disabilities, you can encourage your church to make the needed accommodations, all the while helping leaders through your grace-filled patience with the steep learning curve involved in accommodating the unique needs of your child.

Ownership and Responsibility

Skillful, holistic intervention and accommodations for individuals with mental health disorders can promote a high level of functioning for those with hidden disabilities. As stated previously, a church environment conducive for healing is an environment of loving acceptance and humility, devoid of judgment. Such an environment, however, does *not* preclude acknowledgment of the relational and positional consequences that exist for adults who refuse help. Those who suffer with mental health disorders have responsibility for their behaviors. They must own their challenges and limitations. In cases when they do not, church leaders and Christian friends bear no responsibility for the consequences that impact those who do not take personal ownership or responsibility for their mental health problems.

A woman in a church I once attended liked the attention she drew by telling sordid, fictitious stories about the pastor and fabricated liaisons he purportedly had with parishioners. Her mental health issues wrongly led some parishioners to continue to entertain her stories out of compassion, not wanting to be rude to her. After adequate warnings to stop that went unheeded, church leaders decided to dismiss the woman permanently from attending the church. This woman *chose* not to moderate her conversation topics or receive the help offered her by church leadership. She refused to take ownership or responsibility for her mental health issues. In this case, the church exercised wisdom by removing the welcome mat to her.

Christ-like compassion is always in order. But there are times when God-given discernment tells us to steer clear of a person with a mental health disorder, especially when the one suffering abdicates personal responsibility for aberrant behaviors and invites others to join in with unnecessary drama. In these situations, the mercy hearted within the church have to be especially aware of the need for healthy boundaries. Once again, it is a matter of clergy and church members being educated to the needs and issues of those among them who struggle with mental illnesses.

One way for church leaders and parishioners to obtain a clear perspective on the scope of personal responsibility and thus necessary boundaries toward those with mental health issues is to compare the accountability of a person struggling with mental illness to that of a church member who has a physical impairment such as diabetes. A person with diabetes who willfully lives in complete denial of his body chemistry problems sooner or later suffers the consequences. Eventually his kidneys shut down, and he ends up in a diabetic coma. All an observing believer can do in this case, beyond praying, is to grieve and call 911! Likewise, those with mental illnesses who ignore their symptoms and do not take responsibility for their behaviors do not warrant perpetual involvement from onlookers. Ownership and responsibility of their condition rest with the ones who are ill, not with those around them.

Personally I try to do my best to encourage others to seek treatment and to learn to live with *any* limitations. But ultimately, whether mentally ill, healthy, or ill with some other malady, every individual must make the defining choices for his or her life. And failure to take ownership and personal responsibility has consequences for all people.

A Different Outcome

I'm committed to a different outcome for my progeny than exclusion from church or society due to lack of ownership and taking personal responsibility for their own lives. I'm teaching my children how to self-accommodate. I'm teaching my children how to self-advocate. I'm teaching my children to walk with their heads held high, without shame for disorders they must live with that they did not order off of God's creation menu. But at the same time, I'm contending for my children's healing.

God *can* heal a mental health disorder just as God can miraculously heal cancer or any other condition: physical, emotional, or spiritual. In the last three months, the arthritis I suffered with for over a decade *has disappeared*. Whether the missing symptoms are remission without treatment or a divine healing, I do not know. But I give glory to God for my relief! It encourages me to continue to believe for healing for my children as well.

I know a child who was in the last stages of bone cancer as a toddler when Jesus walked into her bedroom and healed her one hundred percent. She is a young woman now, serving God through Youth With a Mission (YWAM). I worship a God who performs miracles; He displays His power among the peoples (Psalm 77:14 NIV). But for today, I am still living with the reality of sub-optimal brain chemistry in two out of three of my children.

(One important consideration: if you believe you or your child has been miraculously healed of mental illness, do not abruptly cease brain chemistry medication as an act of faith. Allow your psychiatrist to monitor symptoms and slowly titrate medicines down as needed to avoid serious and dangerous medical repercussions.)

While praying for a miracle, I actively pursue interventions for my children with a holistic approach. For example, I ensure a psychiatrist addresses my daughter's underlying neurological condition. I provide counseling, not to cure her mental illness, but to equip her to process through her challenges productively. If she can avoid unforgiveness, shame, bitterness, self-loathing, and other unhealthy coping responses to her suffering, then fewer doors are open for demonic oppression. And I pray the blood of Jesus over my daughter to protect her while contending for her relief and the fulfillment of her destiny. I know the plans God has for my daughter, plans to prosper her, to give her a future and a hope (Jeremiah 29:11).

The churches I have attended throughout the years have met *my* needs but not necessarily the needs of my children. Sometimes it seems the church at large up until very recently has been no better than Job's friends who argued that Job's guilt was responsible for his maladies. It is God who defended Job. And it is God who requires all people be treated with dignity and respect in places of worship. People with mental health issues need the freedom to disclose their special needs if they require any accommodations. And parents raising children with hidden disabilities also need that freedom.

Some mental illness challenges are a lifetime struggle. Raising children with hidden disabilities, when those disabilities are related to mental health, means loving them, helping them, and advocating for them as they struggle and learn to self-advocate. Mental health issues are not just a hidden disability for our children. They are also a hidden challenge for many adults, including those who gather in churches to worship and share life together as the community of Christ.

Reflective Prayer

Heavenly Father,

Empower me to be an advocate within the church to help its people have vision for inclusiveness and the creation of a safe environment. I want others to discover for those with hidden disabilities that You are the God who comforts, encourages, refreshes, and cheers the depressed and sinking (2 Corinthians 7:6 AMP). Reveal Yourself as the One who sees, loves, and heals.

I declare it is You who gives life to our mortal bodies through Your Spirit (Romans 8:11). While each of us with our abilities and disabilities eagerly await the redemption of our bodies (Romans 8:23 NIV), Holy Spirit helps us with our infirmities (Romans 8:26 KJV). Thank You for predestining all of us to be conformed to the image of Your Son (Romans 8:29 NIV). In Jesus' name I pray these words. Amen.

Chapter Thirteen

Ascending the Holy Mountain

Raising children with hidden disabilities can feel like an alpine ascent with no summit finish line in sight. Raising them to know the God of Mount Zion as I do is the peak experience.

A few weeks after my son was diagnosed in kindergarten with the same mental health condition as his older sister, I took the family skiing. He threw a dramatic fit in the parking lot over a minor complaint concerning his hat. I lost my composure, sobbing in great disproportion to my son's offense as I stood there on the snow-covered asphalt at Copper Mountain. It was as though at that very moment I had received the news of his diagnosis.

I suddenly felt like I had been scaling a huge mountain. I was just making enough headway to gain some hope with raising my daughter, when instantly I was teleported back to the parking lot trailhead, only to begin again with my son in tow. At that moment, what seemed like the futility of all my parenting efforts hit me like an avalanche. Memories of using carefully selected words like "Mommy's not strong enough" rather than "you're too heavy" a thousand times when my daughter crumpled and demanded I carry her pelted me like a hailstorm. I'd persevered with these words and ways well into her elementary years. Other exhausting recollections came down on me at the same time.

By the grace of God, I did not allow the blizzard that assailed my mind to define the day that awaited us as a family, eager to ski the picturesque slopes before us. In moments like these, my resiliency comes from a deeply personal, revelatory knowledge of the character and goodness of God.

> In moments like these, my resiliency comes from a deeply personal, revelatory knowledge of the character and goodness of God.

The Character of God Revealed

I recall an earlier instance when God's character revealed brought definition to my life experience of Him. When my father was dying of cancer, the Lord spoke to my brother and gave him strategy for intercession for my father's salvation. Since my brother attended a mainline denomination church and was not particularly charismatic doctrinally, his proclamation about hearing the voice of God got my attention. In response, my siblings and I each obtained friends faithful and gifted in prayer to cover us in intercession for this specific need as we also fervently prayed for my father to come to Christ.

My girls were very young when my father became ill, and he lived five hundred miles away from my family. So with assurance from my father's doctor, I delayed visiting him for a week. Christmas was only a few days away, and I felt I needed to be home with my children for the holiday. My father died the day after Christmas, and to my family's knowledge, he did so without Christ.

When the news came, I felt anger at missing my last opportunity to be with my father and talk with him again about salvation. My flesh wanted to rail against God, to accuse the God I had implored for wisdom as to when I should visit. But my heart couldn't because I had internalized too deeply the character of God. Accusations hurled by the enemy at my heart, lies deriding God, slipped off my spirit like water on Teflon.

I didn't demand answers from God to questions like, "Why did we go to so much trouble with intercessory strategy if my dad was just going to die and go to hell anyway?" Of course, no one knows what transpires in a man's mind as he nears death. My father may well have repented, like the thief on the cross, at the last possible moment. So my heart was quiet and did not demand answers to the why questions.

Not long after returning home from the memorial service, as I sat in a women's prayer group, thinking about unrelated ideas, Holy Spirit spoke and answered the question I hadn't asked. What He spoke was, "Love." With that one word, a cascade of meaning and relevance hit me as though paragraphs were spoken audibly.

A *eureka* may be a better term than a *word* for what transpired. Holy Spirit revealed to me this: God loved my father while my father was still a sinner. God's knowledge that my father would or would not repent did not change God's all-encompassing love for my father because God never gives up. My siblings and I were created in God's image and reflect that image more accurately as we each surrender our will to God, looking more like God in our attitudes and responses. We had devoted that period of time to intercede for my father for the same reason God had inspired the intercession. The reason for the intercession was that God desperately loved my father, even more than my brother, my sister, or I did.

I already had knowledge of God's character and love through studying God's Word, line upon line. But that revelatory moment cemented my knowledge of the character of God even more deeply, knowledge I would need in future years to thwart demands for answers concerning my children.

And so, belayed by the love of God, I continued to make careful word choices with my children, successfully scrambling up the mountain of parenting. My desire was to respond to rages with patience, to teach, to teach, and to teach. I taught when no one, to all appearances, was "home" directing my children's internal compass, the compass that differentiated between reasonable and unreasonable. I kept hiking that mountain.

Just a few years ago, I hiked my first actual fourteener, a mountain that ascends over fourteen thousand feet above sea level. I did so with my teenage son and husband. Mt. Bierstadt is one of Colorado's easier mountains to conquer; yet as we neared the thin air of the summit, the last one and a half hours of trudging necessitated I literally take ten steps, breathe ten breaths, take ten steps, and breathe ten breaths, my single focus on reaching that summit. I made it to the summit, and you will too as you raise your children, contending for their destinies.

> I made it to the summit, and you will too as you raise your children, contending for their destinies.

Sweet Memories That Signal the Summit in Sight

Most of my extended family, a great source of love and comfort to me, lives in the East. By structuring travel to accommodate the needs of the children, my family accomplished the yearly, extended car rides to visit them. We drove less than five hours a day and scheduled a fun reward event at the end of each drive. Over the years, we visited zoos, museums, places of historical interest, and parks across the country.

When my daughter who struggles with brain chemistry was of junior high age, we stopped for the night at a hotel while on one of our family's many summer trips. That night my son vehemently refused to put away his pool toys after playing. My daughter had a flash of lucidness, and she processed through the situation with reason and maturity that left me stunned. It was as though the screen of mental illness had lifted momentarily, and every bit of her absorption of parenting had become clearly visible. I was in shock and enthralled at the same time. I realized that when her chemistry shifted, this child's understanding of right and wrong was indeed intact. My parenting *was* getting through, and it was *not* an exercise in futility.

I desired to parent well, even when there was no evidence my daughter was benefitting. When hope was scarce, I motivated myself by saying I would do all that was motherly possible for my daughter's sake. I reasoned that if the day ever came in adulthood when life crashed and burned for my daughter due to her choices, I could live with myself, knowing that at least my hands were clean. I did not add to my baby's already heavy weight the task of bearing my own frustrations or poor responses to her. I loved her well; I did everything I could for a good outcome. And I believed that eventually culpability would shift; my daughter would make her own life decisions.

That thinking kept me from caving during those really bad seasons when my flesh wanted to respond with retribution rather than grace. After each of those huge scenes with my daughter throwing furniture, screaming, and yelling, I was still the parent when it was over, still the one to do the right thing in response. And my daughter had to feel safe with me, even if I had not felt safe in her presence. I had to be as above reproach as possible.

The irony of those memories is that my child may not remember the hellish scenes she generated, but she may never forget careless words I spoke in my frustration, the one unfair accusation I made against her, and the rough handling she received when it was needed.

To keep myself steady in my parenting choices, I created an invisible audience in my mind to witness the scenes she created, an audience consisting of the family psychiatrist, other family members, life-giving friends from the family's environment of faith, and whomever else I could visualize that might be able to observe objectively with me. My real audience, however, was God, the Lover of my soul, and sometimes my other children or my husband. All of my audiences, real or imagined, caused me to feel a greater sense of accountability as each scene unfolded.

As an adult, my daughter is not bitter against me now for the parenting required to raise her. She truly doesn't remember many of the incidents that preceded calling the police or those multiple evenings spent in the ER for sustained rages. But what she does remember is the many times I held her, the way I believed in her, and my genuine repentance before her when I messed up.

I did not justify my own aberrant behaviors by contrasting them to hers, as though somehow her behaviors made my indiscretions acceptable. And my husband modeled for me contrition skills as a man who owns his mistakes and humbly seeks forgiveness. Together, through all those difficult years, my husband and I hoped our daughter would offer us the same grace we offered her during her childhood. So now, most of our memories are sweet, punctuated by moments of resolution.

Firsthand Revelation on the Holy Mountain

There comes a point in our children's lives when their faith needs to transfer from the faith of parents to their own personal walk with Christ. Their faith must become independent of parents' teachings and also any presumed parental failures they perceive. Watching my children struggle through this season into the next can cause uneasiness as evidence of their "slipping from grace" sends out alarms. I won't have them at home much longer, and I believe they need to be strongly established in their faith prior to leaving home.

> There comes a point in our children's lives when their faith needs to transfer from the faith of parents to their own personal walk with Christ.

The American church is first class in promoting godly character qualities, including integrity, and esteeming knowledge through study. The church in general is weak, however, in experiencing God firsthand in revelatory and dramatic ways that reflect the power of God. This lack is magnified in the lives of the children of our Christian communities, who need more than theology and a tradition of faith to buy into Christianity.

It is not unusual for children to have their first impassioned spiritual experiences at church camp or on short-term mission trips, away from their parents but in life-giving church contexts. When children are known to struggle with behavior due to their hidden disabilities during routine church meetings, few groups welcome them to join the events that are designed to foster deeper intimacy with God. Such exclusions minimize chances for them to see anything beyond the "boring (or sometimes 'entertaining') church as usual" they encounter in their home church environment or household. The result is they have little experiential knowledge of God that convinces them of God's actual very real presence and power.

Forging a pathway for faith in my children has required more than godly instruction, being faithful, and living with integrity behind the scenes. My children have experienced testimonies from multiple guests from developing nations in our home about power encounters with God and the demonic realm, healings, and other overt, supernatural experiences. In spite of these testimonies, my children still need their *own* firsthand revelation of God. Why? Because what my children have seen and heard at home about life in Christ is opposed on every other front: school, friends, required academic reading, video game messages, Hollywood, and Internet exposure.

My prayer for my children is that each one will receive a dramatic, firsthand revelation of God, propelling them into personal intimacy with the Most High that will provide for them a lifetime of purpose and joy in experiencing God. Additionally, I pray that such revelation will transform their relationship with me as their parent—from one of seeing me through eyes of critical evaluation to one that is worthy of their empathy and intercession on my behalf. This transformation has already happened with my firstborn. I wait expectantly for the others.

Saved or Not?

Waiting for your children to embrace God, their Creator and the Lover of their souls, may send you back to the journals of theology, wondering if their childhood profession of faith was real. You may question if your son understood enough of the gospel to make his salvation experience legitimate. You may wonder if your daughter knew the significance of what she was praying when she dutifully recited prayers for forgiveness of sins. If you have "once saved, always saved" dogma, the question is critical as you watch them as teens, renouncing all those years of Christian indoctrination.

I can still remember standing by the coats in the cloakroom of my Methodist church's preschool, listening to my teacher explain the gospel. She later led me in the Sinner's Prayer. I knew I was saved after that, although my mother insists I had prayed with her many times previously to be saved. Those times I cannot recall, yet that scene in the preschool is where I felt the transaction made in heaven. Scripture teaches that unless we change and become like little children, we cannot inherit the Kingdom of heaven (Matthew 18:3). So yes, I believe children's professions of faith are valid.

Once I began to study the Word of God on my own as a young woman, I encountered some tricky passages in the book of Hebrews and elsewhere that caused me to evaluate my own faith. I saw myself in those pages more like the Israelites, falling away repetitively and following after God more for the benefits of the faith than for God Himself. Although born and raised in the church, it occurred to me that I had reason to question my salvation.

It wasn't that I thought I was not saved at all. Instead, I likened my experience to that of taking a screening test for cancer and miserably failing it. In this story line, it didn't mean that I actually had cancer, but that I would be a fool if I didn't follow through to get more testing to evaluate whether or not there was a problem. The risk was too great to ignore. So I began to inspect the fruit in my life.

I believed in God. I mean, I *really* believed in God. I heard His voice audibly once as a child. I believed Jesus was God's Son, God in the flesh, and was able to die in my stead to pay the price for my sins precisely because Jesus was without sin. Did my beliefs, cemented by dramatic moments hearing and later experiencing God in other ways, mean I was "saved" from paying for my own sins through the second death, which was hell and eternal separation from God? A verse I'd read in the book of James came back to me. "You say you have faith, for you believe that there is one God. Good for you! Even the demons believe this, and they tremble in terror" (James 2:19).

Demons are not "saved" as Christians understand the term. But I venture to guess, by the description of them trembling in terror, that they may fear the Lord even more than I do at times. The difference is in lordship. Demons do not submit their wills to the Lord Jesus Christ. Mere *knowing* the identity of Christ does not produce salvation; rather, positioning oneself in submission to Christ's lordship as the propitiation through His blood for sins produces salvation. It is an act many professing believers have never done in spite of *saying* they have repented.

Some who call themselves Christians have retained the "right" to be their own bosses. They call their self-will "grace." But the true grace of God is not license to sin (Jude 1:4). The true grace of God allows you and me to live in triumph over sin through Christ (Romans 5:17). Neither position is sinless, but one retains the right to sin. The other yields to God and to His right to rule over our lives, trusting in the blood of Jesus to cleanse us from all sin.

The rich young ruler portrayed in Matthew 19:16–26 probably had no objection to asking for forgiveness for his sins, either again or for the first time in his life. But he did object to unequivocal submission of his life to a higher authority. He walked away from Jesus, grieving and understanding the cost of commitment.

I asked for forgiveness of my sins when I was only four years old. But years later, I placed Christ on the throne of my life, making Him my ultimate authority. Perhaps the moment I surrendered my will to God is when it could be said that I was *really* saved.

All three of my children made professions of faith in their early childhoods. When my middle daughter was only in kindergarten, she could not contain her enthusiasm and zeal for God, the Miracle Worker. Once she prayed on her own initiative for the healing of her plantar warts, warts that had spread over the preceding few years into painful mosaics that covered the ball of her foot. The very next morning after her earnest petition, the warts disappeared completely, without a trace.

Today my daughter has no recollection of this profound event. But she does recall the many prayers she has prayed for relief of depression, anxiety, obsessions, and tics; and she has decided God doesn't exist after all. For today.

Age of Accountability

Another question that burdens me about the spiritual life of my children is, "At what age are my children with hidden disabilities culpable for their sin?" Scripture does not explicitly teach there's an age of accountability whereby one is old enough to choose to trust in Christ's provision in order to be saved or experience the consequences of choosing differently.

King David, a man steeped in revelation, stopped fasting and praying after hearing his sick baby had died (2 Samuel 12:22). David believed his child was with God, not burning in the fire of hell. He didn't want to lose his child from the earth, but he did not seem to be concerned about the child's afterlife (in spite of the fact that theologically all mankind is born into sin). David even said of himself, "Surely I was sinful at birth, sinful from the time my mother conceived me" (Psalm 51:5 NIV). In other words, he believed a baby did not have to live for any amount of time to sin in order to be considered a sinner. Sin, he declared, is an inherited condition.

From this story, I can extrapolate that there is an age in which I can no longer be so sure my children have a ticket into heaven without evidence of concomitant repentance. But what is that age? And is it different for every child? At the magical age of sixteen, American teens are deemed of adequate sound mind and maturity to be granted a driver's license. But wise parents know better and delay licensure for those children who are slower developmentally than the average child. So then, can I expect God to make determinations on a case-by-case basis for when my children become accountable for their sins?

One thing I do know. I am raising my children for eternity and not just for their short stint here on earth. I take comfort in knowing that I prayed about my children's salvation even while they were still infants. And I have wondered which is ultimately more devastating to a parent: to lose a young child to death or to lose adult progeny to hell, which means eternal separation. I held this question near to my heart when my babies were young, hoping I would never need it as a comfort if the unthinkable were to happen. I never want to be separated from my children, not now and not later.

Here's a more difficult question. How much are my children spiritually accountable for when they have oppositional defiant brain chemistry? When they can't seem to submit to the simplest instructions on some days, how can they submit to God? I liken my children's submission to the rich man's unlikelihood of surrender. Jesus told His disciples it was easier for a camel to go through the eye of a needle than for a rich man to enter the Kingdom of God. But then Jesus exclaimed, "Humanly speaking it is impossible. But with God everything is possible." (Matthew 19:23–26). So I choose to believe in the impossible.

Climbing the mountain of parenting, which includes leading our children up the Holy Mountain, may not be so difficult after all. I can believe what Jesus said, "I tell you the truth, if you have faith and don't doubt. . . . You can even say to this mountain, 'May you be lifted up and thrown into the sea,' and it will happen" (Matthew 21:21). I can be as Zerubbabel and declare that nothing, not even a mighty mountain, will stand in my way; it will become a level plain before me, in Jesus' Name (Zechariah 4:7).

Reflective Prayer

Heavenly Father,

I surrender my right to be my own boss. I want the true grace of the Lord Jesus Christ to empower me to "live in triumph" (Romans 5:17). I no longer allow myself the option of sin because of how I am feeling in the moment. I surrender my right to hold on to anger, bitterness, and unforgiveness, asking for Your grace to empower me to do so. I trust in the blood of Jesus to be the payment for my sins before a God of both justice and merciful love.

Forgive me for all the ways I have fallen short of Your righteous standard. I stand clean and forgiven before You, dressed in the righteousness of my Jesus. I declare that I have received the Spirit that I may "know the things freely given" me by God (1 Corinthians 2:12 NASB).

Just as I desire for myself, I also ask that each of my children receive a dramatic, firsthand revelation of You. Propel them into personal intimacy with You that provides them a lifetime of purpose and joy in experiencing You. In Jesus' name I pray these words. Amen.

Chapter Fourteen

Contending for Destiny

Jane Hamon of Christian International Ministries told of a vision she had of a boxing ring.[24] There was a contender in the ring named Devourer. No one challenged him! As Jane was wondering why no one entered the ring to fight, the boxer turned around, and she read the embroidery on the robe across his back: "That's Just Life."

Before I had children, I told the Lord I wanted world changers. I wasn't looking for compliant, easy-to-raise babies. But during those roughest years with my daughter when she was having rage attacks, getting expelled from schools, and spending time in psychiatric hospitals, the "beatings" lowered my sights. It wasn't long, however, before I re-entered the ring and discarded my "That's Just Life" robe. I'm contending for my rightful inheritance in Christ, my children's destinies.

The fight you are engaged in is for a reason, or even reasons yet to be revealed. The Bible's language for this fight is "fiery trials" (1 Peter 4:12). "The crucible is for refining silver and the furnace is for gold, likewise the LORD tests hearts" (Proverbs 17:3 NET Bible). The same fire that consumes stubble purifies gold. The result of fire in your life is solely dependent upon your own constitution, not the source of that fire as being from heaven or hell. The significance of that observation lies in the putting to rest the question of origin, "Did God allow my child to have this disability, or is the trial straight from the pit of hell?"

The victories ahead are dependent upon your character and constitution, formed and reformed by the fire. Through raising children with hidden disabilities, you are being refined to shine forth love that is unconditional. You are becoming excellent at patience. You are learning to see beneath your children's pathologies and brokenness from life's experiences to the people God created them to be. Perhaps most importantly, you are modeling to the world how to walk in compassion and not judgment.

Refinement

Your refinement is teaching you to be in charge of the atmosphere rather than to become a victim of it. You can turn situations around for the positive. You can see that which is good, priceless, and valuable, no matter how obscured. For the people of this world who have lost so much of themselves through sin and destructive behaviors, you have a redemptive vision. You

> Your refinement is teaching you to be in charge of the atmosphere rather than to become a victim of it.

are becoming more and more able to spot, affirm, and call out the truth to the lost, the disenfranchised. Through your refinement, they will see their true identity and potential, emerging from the ground like a spring crocus. Your salvation and refinement through Jesus Christ will lead them to theirs.

My daughter too is being refined like gold through the fire. She has learned to stand strong in the face of rejection, cruel judgment, and the absence of friends over long seasons. She has suffered through verbal attacks of other children against her and misunderstandings. She has cried over the pain of those who don't realize their own value, those ensnared by drugs and promiscuity, classmates who were less committed to her than she was to them. She has been rejected in church by peers and unloved by adults who were inconvenienced by her.

My daughter's years of pain and isolation have given her time to explore the world's social ills, the condition of mankind, and the fallen nature of humanity. She is a deep well, knowing sorrow and elation. She is passionate about the marginalized and social justice. My daughter is motivated by love, as is Jesus in the provision of the gospel.

I love the woman my daughter is becoming, just as I loved the child she was at one time. Medication was never for the purpose of changing my daughter so that she would be easier to raise. I stopped drug trials of medications that made her more manageable but altered her personality. I *liked* her, and was not willing to lose *her*. Her at her best was always my desire.

The interventions we choose for our children are about calling them into their destinies, peeling off the negatives of their disabilities while rejoicing in the positives. These interventions are also about training in strategies to move forward toward inner productivity and expression of their truest selves. And they are about actualization of our children's many gifts and talents. All interventions at their core are about freeing our children to experience the beauty of life, relationships, and redemption. They empower our children to benefit from the refinement that redeems their suffering.

The Process

When I read about the life of King David in retrospect, it is easy to see there was not shame in his waiting years in spite of the struggles and faltering. He must not have felt very kingly as he feigned insanity before the King of Gath (1 Samuel 21). He must not have felt kingly when he drew the discontents to himself and hid with them in caves (1 Samuel 22). "Becoming" is a process, a process that is not always glamorous in the making.

The psalmist says in Psalm 119 (NIV), "My soul is weary with sorrow; strengthen me according to your word (v. 28) and also, "I am laid low in the dust; preserve my life according to your word" (v. 25). In that same chapter the psalmist says, "You are my refuge and my shield" (v. 114) and, "I rise before dawn and cry for help; I have put my hope in your word" (v. 147). These verses show me that the *process of becoming* is facilitated by God, who is a strengthener, a preserver, a refuge, a shield, and the source of hope.

Romans 4:3 says, "Abraham believed God, and it was credited to him as righteousness" (NIV). Abraham did not become righteous the moment he retroactively received the promises God made to him. Additionally, David did not become worthy of respect the moment he attained position of king. The fight David endured to reach his destiny prepared him for greatness. The journey for Abraham and David was no less significant than the moment of attainment.

The battle that parents of children with hidden disabilities and the battle the children themselves fight prepare them for destiny. Each skirmish of the battle is different, but in every case, the contender can come from a position of strength. May it be said with confidence, just as Job proclaimed, "When he has tested me, I will come forth as gold" (Job 23:10 NIV).

> **The battle that parents of children with hidden disabilities and the battle the children themselves fight prepare them for destiny.**

Promises

I live in Colorado, home to predator mountain lions, bobcats, emboldened coyotes, and even bears right in my neighborhood. Late one evening when my daughter was young, she went into a rage and took off running into the greenbelt of wilderness that serpentines through the houses in my neighborhood. Night was falling, and when it did, I knew safety would become a more serious issue. Rather than come home, she would likely hunker down in the same places as would wildlife. She had no flashlight or jacket for the cool evening air.

My husband called the police, and the local heat-seeking security helicopter eventually flushed my child out of the dark woods, floodlights blazing. After the authorities subjected her to a mandatory fingerprinting like a criminal, we were free to go home and process through the day's events. Throughout this drama, I kept my sanity by reminding myself that I had promises concerning this child.

The revelation God has given me through His Word concerning His good intentions for my child undergirds my faith when crises like this one seem to contradict His intended destiny for her. God's good intentions have not changed as my daughter has grown into a young woman. Yet God does not override my daughter's own will or force His best on her. My daughter does not embrace Christianity at this stage in her life, but I remain content in knowing my children must discover their own faith rather than embrace an extension of mine.

As a young adult now, my daughter sees great injustices in the world even though she doesn't share my conviction relating to the true source of human suffering. Determined to do something to right the wrongs, she embraces humanism, feminism, homosexual rights, and anything that radically claims to combat the conditions of the world. For this season in her life, my daughter is more concerned with humanity's condition than God's heart.

I have already had a trial run of remaining at peace while my daughter ventures into the dark among predators. I pray for the penetrating light of God to flush her out, but ultimately it is her choice to face the arduous walk home on her own accord. As I wait, my peace comes from the promises of God.

Right now my daughter's biggest challenge is mastering the debilitating effects of brain chemistry that have left her severely disadvantaged, fighting contenders named Anxiety and Depression. It's not ideal watching ringside while my child battles, but the ideal is one idol I have successfully toppled.

I remind God that I have raised each of my children up in the way that they should go, and I stand on the proverbial promise that eventually they will not depart from it (Proverbs 22:6). In the meantime, I love them all the same as they figure out life. I honor the process while contending for their destiny.

Reflective Prayer

Heavenly Father,

"I could have no greater joy than to hear that my children are following the truth" (3 John 1:4). Sometimes "I feel as if I am going through labor pains" for them all over again, and that pain "will continue until Christ is fully developed" in each one of their lives (Galatians 4:19).

I know it's not just me that earnestly intercedes for my children. Jesus Himself is their advocate before You, Father (1 John 2:1).

"Listen to my cry for help, my King and my God, for I pray to no one but you" (Psalm 5:2). I stand on Your promise that You show love to a thousand generations of those who love You and keep Your commandments (Exodus 20:6 NIV). I am committed to train up each of my children in the way they should go. By the power of the blood of the Lord Jesus Christ, I decree that when they are old, not a single one of my children will depart from Your ways (Proverbs 22:6 NASB). In Jesus' name I pray these words. Amen.

About the Author

After a stint in Bible college, two community colleges, and a university in Florida, Melanie Boudreau graduated highest honors from the University of Texas, School of Allied Health, with a degree in medical technology. As an ASCP certified medical technologist, Melanie expected an exciting career in the health field. Instead, she soon discovered that parenting was an even greater passion. The mother of one child who was neurotypical and two with neuropsychiatric disorders, Melanie used her education to interact with specialists and to research interventions for her children.

Meanwhile, Melanie earns an income working as a Team Director for Apostolic Intercessors Network, a Christian business that links professional level intercessors and spiritual warfare strategists with individuals, families, and workplace leaders around the globe. She loves traveling, hiking, skiing, camping, and Hungarian puli dogs. Melanie has been happily married for over thirty years and has a grandson named Brave.

Notes

Foreword

1   http://www.ist.hawaii.edu/training/hiddendisabilities/05_hidden_disabilities.php

2   http://www.ist.hawaii.edu/training/hiddendisabilities/05_hidden_disabilities.php

Chapter One

3   http://www.amazon.com/What-Makes-Ryan-Tick-Hyperactivity/dp/1878267353

4   http://www.amazon.com/The-Explosive-Child-Understanding-Chronically/dp/0061906190

Chapter Six

5   http://drgrcevich.wordpress.com

6   Stephen Grcevich, MD, "What's Causing the Epidemic of Mental Illness in Kids?" *Key Ministry* May 6, 2014 *Church4EveryChild* http://drgcevich.wordpress.com/2014/05/06/whats-causing-the-epidemic-of-mental-illness-in-kids-2/ (May 30, 2014).

7   http://www.tv.com/shows/monk/

8   "History of Autism Blame" *Refrigerator Mothers* July 16, 2002 *POV Documentaries with a Point of View* http://www.pbs.org/pov/refrigeratormothers.fridge.php (June 06, 2014).

Chapter Seven

9   Rick Nauert, PhD, "Brain Changes from Child Abuse Tied to Adult Mental Illness, Sexual Problems," June 3, 2013, *PsychCentral Learn. Share. Grow.* http://psychcentral.com/news/2013/06/03/brain-changes-from-child-abuse-tied-to-adult-mental-illness-sexual-problems/55556.html#at_pco=smlre-1.0&at_si=53801c7cfff921e7&at_ab=per-3&at_pos (May 30, 2014).

10 Ashton Action, PhD, General Editor, *Traumatic Stress Disorders: New Insights for the Healthcare Professional* (2012 Edition: A Scholarly Editions™ Scholarly Paper™. Copyright © 2012 by Scholarly Editions™).

11 http://vcoy.virginia.gov/collection.asp

12 http://www.genomind.com

13 Daniel G. Amen, MD, *Change Your Brain Change Your Life.* (New York: Random House, 1998).

14 Daniel G. Amen, MD, "Mapping the Brain: Creating Advantages in Psychiatric Care: The Advantages of Brain SPECT Imaging With Complex Psychiatric Patients" 2014, *Dorland Health* http://www.dorlandhealth.com/dorland-health-articles/CIP_0113_14_Depressionxml (May 30, 2014).

15 http://ods.od.nih.gov

Chapter Eight

16 Peter W.D. Wright and Pamela Darr Wright. *Wrightslaw: Special Education Law,* 2nd ed. (Hartfield, Va.: Harbor House Law Press, 2007).

17 Peter W.D. Wright and Pamela Darr Wright. *Wrightslaw: From Emotions to Advocacy : The Special Education Survival Guide,* 2nd ed. (Hartfield, Va.: Harbor House Law Press, 2006).

18 http://www.wrightslaw.com

19 Theresa Sidebotham, "Educating Children with Disabilities—Navigating the Maze" *Special Education Clickapedia* 28 February 2014 *Telios Law PLLC http://telioslaw.com/clickapedia-on-special-education* (14 June 2014).

Chapter Eleven

20 American Hindu Foundation. "Yoga Beyond Asana: Hindu Thought In Practice." http://hafsite.org/media/pr/yoga-hindu-origins (accessed August 3, 2014).

Chapter Twelve

21 John M. Grohol, Psy.D. Mental Health Statistics *World of Psychology* 3 May 2010 *PsychCentral: Learn. Share. Grow http://psychcentral.com/blog/archives/2010/05/03/mental-health-statistics/* (15 June 2014).
22 http://drgrcevich.wordpress.com
23 http://www.keyministry.org

Chapter Fourteen

24 Jane Hamon. Lecture, Awakening 2013 Ministers & Leaders Summit from Christian International, Santa Rosa Beach, February 26, 2013.

Made in the USA
Middletown, DE
10 November 2015